CARIBBEAN CRUISE
PORTS HANDBOOK
2025

JASON H. FORD

Copyright © 2024 by Jason H. Ford

All rights reserved. No part of this book may be reproduced, distributed, or transmitted in any form or by any means, including photocopying, recording, or other electronic or mechanical methods, without the prior written permission of the publisher, except in the case of brief quotations embodied in critical reviews and specific other noncommercial uses permitted by copyright law

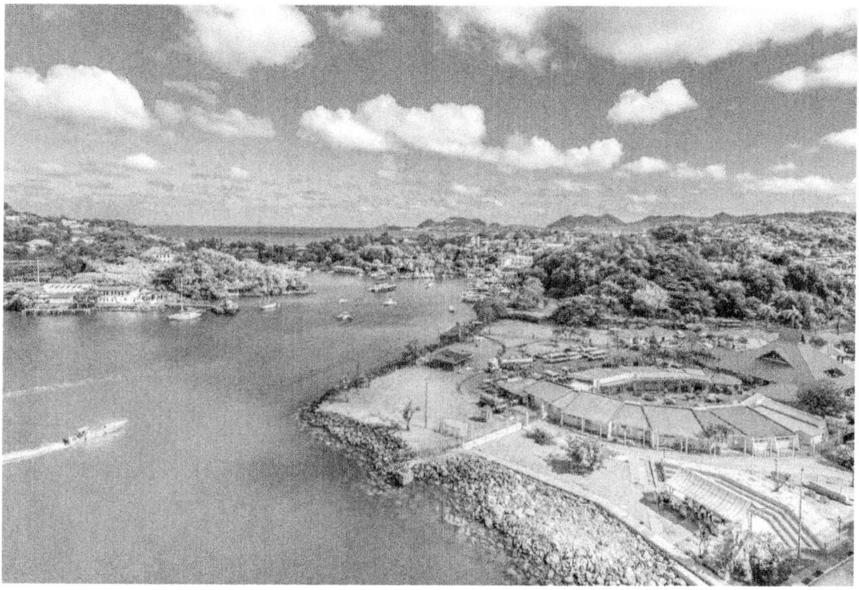

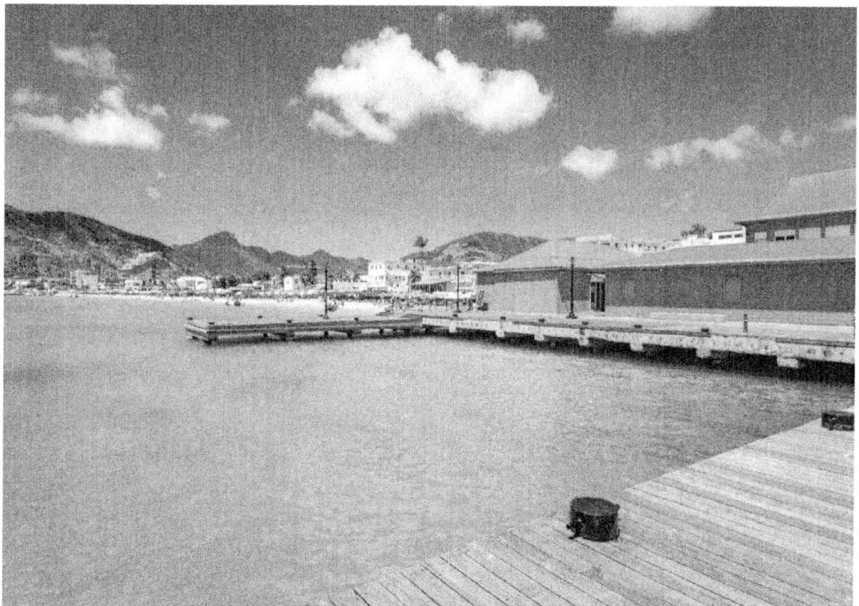

TABLE OF CONTENTS

INTRODUCTION 7
   Overview of the Caribbean 10
   Why Choose a Caribbean Cruise 12
   What to Expect 15
CHAPTER 1 18
PLANNING YOUR TRIP 18
   Packing and planning 18
   Best Times to Cruise 20
   Duration of your trip 24
   Caribbean Cruise a budget 26
   Choosing the right Cruise Line 29
   Entry and visa requirements 33
CHAPTER 2 37
GETTING TO CARIBBEAN CRUISE DEPARTURE POINT 37
   Caribbean Cruise departure point 37
   : Arrival and Orientation 37
   Journey to Caribbean Cruise Departure points 40
CHAPTER 3 43
EASTERN CARIBBEAN PORTS 43
   Nassau, Bahamas 43
   Philipsburg, St. Maarten 47
   San Juan, Puerto Rico 52
   St. Thomas, U.S. Virgin Islands 57
CHAPTER 4 63
WESTERN CARIBBEAN PORTS 63
   Galveston, Texas 63
   Cozumel, Mexico 67

Costa Maya, Mexico... 72
Grand Cayman, Cayman Islands...77
Belize City, Belize... 81
Ocho Rios, Jamaica..86
Falmouth, Jamaica.. 91
Roatán, Honduras... 95

CHAPTER 5.. 100
SOUTHERN CARIBBEAN PORTS........................... 100
Bridgetown, Barbados...100
Oranjestad, Aruba... 104
Willemstad, Curaçao... 109
St. George's, Grenada...113

CHAPTER 6.. 118
PRIVATE ISLANDS AND EXCLUSIVE STOPS.........118
CocoCay, Bahamas (Royal Caribbean)..............................118
Half Moon Cay, Bahamas (Holland America Line).......... 123
Great Stirrup Cay, Bahamas (Norwegian Cruise Line..... 129
Amber Cove, Dominican Republic (Carnival)................... 133

CHAPTER 7.. 139
EXCURSION AND ADVENTURES........................... 139
Snorkeling and Diving Highlights......................................139
Nature and Wildlife Encounters..141
Adventure Activities: Zip-lining, ATVs, and Hiking........ 144

CHAPTER 8.. 147
BEACH BLISS.. 147
Best Beaches by Region... 147
Secluded vs. Popular Beaches... 149
Tips for a Perfect Beach Day... 152

CHAPTER 9.. 155

CULINARY DELIGHTS..**155**
   Iconic Caribbean Dishes to Try.. 155
   Rum and Local Drinks Guide.. 157
   Best Local Restaurants Near Ports..159
CHAPTER 10..**165**
CRUISE TIPS FOR FIRST-TIMERS.......................**165**
   Maximizing Your Time in Port..165
   Cruise Etiquette and Safety...167
CHAPTER 11..**170**
CARIBBEAN CRUISE PLANNER............................**170**
   Sample Itineraries for Different Interests....................... 170
   Resources and Useful Links.. 173
CHAPTER 12..**176**
PRACTICAL INFORMATION...................................**176**
    Money matters and Currency Exchange.........................176
    Language and Communication...180
    Safety and Health...183
    Emergency Contacts..187
    Useful Websites and Apps... 191
CONCLUSION...**195**
   MAP...198

INTRODUCTION

A Caribbean cruise is more than just a journey; it's a gateway to a world of sun-kissed beaches, diverse cultures, and beautiful scenery. As you cruise across the azure seas of the Caribbean Sea, each wave brings you closer to a kaleidoscope of islands, each with its own distinct charm and fascination. From the rhythmic sounds of reggae in Jamaica to the rich heritage of colonial architecture in San Juan, the Caribbean offers an excursion that tantalizes the senses while rejuvenating the soul.

I still remember the first time I set sail for the Caribbean. My imagination ran wild with images of postcard-perfect beaches and vivid sunsets. But what I found was something deeper—a connection to the heart of each island and its people. My initial goal had been to unwind, to chase the clichés of tropical bliss, but the unexpected came in the form of a friendly local sharing a tale about the island's history, or a quiet cove where I felt entirely at peace. These moments reshaped my understanding of what travel could be.

The first port we docked at welcomed me with the aroma of fresh seafood grilling on the beach and the cheerful sounds of a local band. Everything about it was alive, yet calm—a juxtaposition that made me stop in my tracks. The markets overflowed with handmade crafts and tropical fruits I couldn't name, while fishermen hauled in the day's catch against the backdrop of azure waves. The vibrant atmosphere was intoxicating, but what truly stayed with me were the quieter moments: watching a pelican dive gracefully into the water or walking through a historic town as the golden light of dusk softened its edges.

Exploring the islands felt like opening a treasure chest. There were the iconic spots everyone talks about—the waterfalls, the beaches that seem too perfect to be real—but there were also the tucked-away corners where life unfolded unhurried. I stumbled upon a family-run café where the matriarch cooked her grandmother's recipes and found a winding trail that led to an overlook so breathtaking it felt like standing on the edge of the world. These weren't just destinations; they were stories waiting to be told.

The Caribbean Cruise isn't just a place you visit; it's a place you feel. It's the warmth of the sun on your skin, the salt-laden breeze that carries laughter from the shore, and the unshakable sense of freedom that comes with being surrounded by boundless blue horizons. It's a journey of joy, reflection, and wonder, where every moment becomes a cherished memory.

This travel guide isn't merely a collection of tips and itineraries; it's an invitation. It's a call to immerse yourself in the vibrant tapestry of the Caribbean Cruise, to uncover its secrets and savor its magic. Whether you're planning your first voyage or reliving cherished memories, this guide will help you navigate the highlights, uncover hidden gems, and embrace the essence of each port of call.

So step aboard, let your curiosity set sail, and prepare to fall in love with the Caribbean Cruise. This is your adventure—one that promises discovery, connection, and the kind of beauty that stays with you long after you've returned home.

Overview of the Caribbean

The Caribbean is a region that instantly brings to mind images of turquoise waters, swaying palm trees, and sun-kissed shores. It is a vast expanse of islands and coastal countries, each offering a unique flavor of culture, history, and natural beauty. Stretching from the southeastern coast of the United States to the northern shores of South America, the Caribbean is home to over 7,000 islands, though only a fraction of them are inhabited. From bustling cities to sleepy fishing villages, there's something here for every kind of traveler.

One of the first things you notice in the Caribbean is the diversity. Each island has its own story to tell, shaped by centuries of colonial history, native traditions, and waves of immigrants who brought their own cultures to the mix. You'll find French influences in Guadeloupe and Martinique, Dutch heritage in Curaçao and Aruba, British traditions in Barbados and Jamaica, and Spanish flair in Puerto Rico and the Dominican Republic. This cultural variety extends to the food, language, music, and architecture, making every destination feel like an entirely new adventure.

The natural beauty of the Caribbean is truly mesmerizing. Pristine beaches with soft, white sand are the star attraction for many, but beyond the shoreline, there's so much more to discover. Rainforests, waterfalls, and lush mountains make islands like Dominica and St. Lucia a haven for nature lovers. Coral reefs, teeming with marine life, invite snorkelers and divers to explore an underwater paradise, while clear waters provide the perfect playground for sailing, kayaking, and paddleboarding.

The Caribbean is not just a feast for the eyes but also for the soul. The vibrant energy of the people is infectious. Everywhere you go, there's an air of warmth and joy, whether you're greeted by a local vendor at a market or a guide taking you through a historic fort. Music is the heartbeat of the islands, with rhythms of reggae, calypso, and salsa filling the air, often accompanied by the scent of jerk chicken, fresh seafood, or tropical fruits sizzling on a grill.

Cruising through the Caribbean is one of the best ways to experience the region. Each port of call offers a chance to step into a different world, whether you're wandering through the pastel-colored streets of Old San Juan, hiking to Dunn's River Falls in Jamaica, or lounging on Seven Mile Beach in Grand Cayman. With so much variety, it's impossible to see it all in one trip, but that's part of the magic—there's always another island to look forward to.

The charm of the Caribbean lies in its ability to cater to all kinds of travelers. Whether you're seeking relaxation, adventure, history, or culture, you'll find it here. The laid-back lifestyle of the islands invites you to slow down and savor every moment, creating memories that will stay with you long after the journey ends.

Why Choose a Caribbean Cruise

The allure of the Caribbean cruise ports is undeniable. These vibrant destinations stand out for their rich blend of culture, history, and natural splendor, making them a paradise for explorers and relaxation seekers alike. Whether you're drawn by the promise of golden sands and crystal-clear waters or intrigued by the layered stories of colonial heritage and island resilience, the Caribbean offers an experience that is as diverse as it is enchanting.

Caribbean ports are each unique, from the pastel-colored colonial buildings of Old San Juan to the bustling marketplaces of Bridgetown and the serene coves of Roatán. What sets this region apart is its ability to offer both the familiar comforts of world-class amenities and the exotic charm of unspoiled nature. Many of these ports have preserved their cultural and architectural identity, giving visitors a glimpse into a world shaped by the interplay of European, African, and Indigenous influences.

Among the must-see attractions is Dunn's River Falls in Jamaica, where cascading waters invite adventurous visitors to climb through its natural steps. In Nassau, the Queen's Staircase leads to Fort Fincastle, blending history and breathtaking views. Curaçao's colorful waterfront, lined with Dutch colonial architecture, is a feast for the eyes and an Instagram favorite. For wildlife enthusiasts, St. Lucia's Pitons and Dominica's rainforests offer encounters with lush biodiversity. Meanwhile, the Grand Cayman Sandbar gives travelers the rare opportunity to swim among friendly stingrays in shallow waters.

Cultural immersion is one of the greatest rewards of visiting Caribbean ports. Each island tells its story through music, dance, and traditions that visitors can join. Festivals like the Trinidad and Tobago Carnival or Junkanoo in the Bahamas showcase the region's vibrant spirit with parades, costumes, and infectious rhythms. Markets filled with handcrafted souvenirs and local delicacies invite deeper connections with the communities, while the warmth of the people turns every interaction into a cherished memory.

The natural beauty of the Caribbean is nothing short of spectacular. The islands are home to pristine beaches, coral reefs teeming with marine life, and lush inland rainforests that beckon explorers. Scenic viewpoints like Shirley Heights in Antigua or Mount Liamuiga in St. Kitts reward hikers with panoramic views. For those who prefer water-based activities, snorkeling in Belize's Barrier Reef or kayaking through bioluminescent bays in Puerto Rico creates memories that last a lifetime.

Food lovers will find the Caribbean ports to be a haven of culinary delights. Each island has its signature dishes, from Jamaica's jerk chicken to Barbados' flying fish and cou-cou. Local markets like the Castries Market in St. Lucia or Oistin's Fish Fry in Barbados are perfect for savoring freshly caught seafood and mingling with locals. Beachfront restaurants and cozy eateries often serve dishes infused with spices and ingredients unique to the region, delivering flavors that linger long after the meal.

Visitors often speak of the profound sense of connection they feel while exploring the Caribbean. A seasoned traveler once shared how the rhythm of the steel drums and the scent of salt in the air made her feel instantly at home, while another fondly recounted the simple joy of a beachside coconut water vendor striking up a conversation. These personal moments make the Caribbean not just a destination but an experience of a lifetime.

Traveling to the Caribbean cruise ports is relatively easy, with major ports accessible from North America and Europe. The best times to visit are during the dry season, from December to April, when the weather is warm and sunny. Families will find plenty of activities for kids, while couples can enjoy romantic sunsets and private excursions. Solo travelers will appreciate the welcoming atmosphere and ease of navigation.

These ports deserve a place on every traveler's itinerary for their unmatched combination of natural beauty, cultural richness, and adventure. Each visit unveils something new, from the laughter of children playing by the beach to the timeless melodies of calypso and reggae. Discover the magic for yourself and let the Caribbean leave its mark on your heart.

What to Expect

When visiting the Caribbean, expect to be welcomed by vibrant energy, stunning landscapes, and warm hospitality. The region is known for its laid-back atmosphere, where life moves at a slower, more enjoyable pace. The moment you step off the ship, you'll feel a sense of freedom that comes with leaving behind the stresses of daily life. The Caribbean invites you to immerse yourself in its beauty, culture, and experiences.

The first thing to expect is the stunning natural environment. Picture endless turquoise waters meeting white sandy beaches shaded by palm trees. Some islands boast dramatic cliffs and volcanic peaks, while others are flat and surrounded by lush mangroves. The weather is typically warm and sunny, with gentle ocean breezes adding to the comfort. Be prepared to spend plenty of time outdoors, whether you're lounging by the water, hiking through rainforests, or exploring underwater wonders like coral reefs and colorful fish.

The culture here is as diverse as the islands themselves. Every destination has its unique flavor, shaped by centuries of history and a mix of influences. Expect to hear a variety of languages, from English and Spanish to French and Dutch, depending on where you are. The locals are friendly and eager to share their traditions, whether it's through music, dance, or food. Don't be surprised if you're invited to join in a street festival or try a new dish at a local market. It's all part of the Caribbean charm.

Each port offers its own distinct attractions, so expect every stop on your journey to feel like a new adventure. One day you might find yourself wandering through colorful colonial streets, and the next, you could be snorkeling in a secluded bay. Historic forts, botanical gardens, and cultural museums are common highlights, as are the endless options for water sports and excursions. If you love exploring, you'll have no shortage of options to fill your days with excitement.

Food is a big part of the Caribbean experience, so expect to indulge in a variety of flavors. From savory jerk chicken and fresh seafood to sweet tropical fruits and desserts, there's something to satisfy every palate. Dining ranges from casual beachside shacks to elegant restaurants, giving you the chance to try local favorites in every setting. Don't miss the chance to sip on a freshly made piña colada or sample locally brewed rum—it's all part of embracing the island vibe.

When it comes to shopping, expect a mix of handcrafted souvenirs, vibrant textiles, and local artwork. Many ports have lively markets where you can browse unique items and interact with artisans. These markets are also great spots to pick up spices, jams, or coffee to take a taste of the Caribbean home with you. Remember to leave room in your luggage for these treasures, as they make the perfect reminder of your trip.

The pace of life in the Caribbean is slow and relaxed, so don't expect everything to move as quickly as you might be used to. This is a place where people take time to enjoy the moment, and visitors are encouraged to do the same. Take the opportunity to disconnect from your usual routine and fully embrace the "island time" mentality. It's an adjustment that quickly becomes a highlight of the experience.

Practical things to expect include well-organized tours, friendly guides, and easy access to most attractions. While some ports are bustling and filled with amenities, others are quieter and more off the beaten path. Pack light, comfortable clothing, sunscreen, and water shoes if you plan on exploring waterfalls or rocky shorelines. Remember to keep an open mind and a sense of adventure as you explore.

Above all, expect to leave the Caribbean with a heart full of memories. The beauty of the islands, the richness of the culture, and the warmth of the people combine to create an unforgettable experience. It's a place where every moment feels special, and every visit leaves you longing to return.

CHAPTER 1.
PLANNING YOUR TRIP

Packing and planning

Packing and planning for a Caribbean cruise is an exciting part of the journey, setting the tone for the adventure ahead. With the right preparation, you can ensure a stress-free experience and focus entirely on the fun and beauty that await you. Packing for a cruise is a little different from other trips, so keeping things simple and practical is key. Start by considering the warm Caribbean climate and the activities you'll enjoy, from beach days and island tours to dining on board and exploring bustling ports.

Light, breathable clothing is essential for the Caribbean's tropical weather. Pack plenty of lightweight shorts, dresses, and tops made from materials like cotton or linen. For days spent lounging by the pool or exploring the beaches, include swimsuits, cover-ups, and flip-flops. If you plan on water activities like snorkeling or kayaking, water shoes can come in handy. Don't forget a wide-brimmed hat and sunglasses to protect yourself from the sun while still looking stylish.

Evenings on a cruise often call for slightly dressier outfits, especially if you plan to dine in the ship's main dining room or attend any formal nights. A sundress or smart casual attire will usually suffice, but for formal evenings, men may want a light jacket or tie, and women might enjoy wearing a cocktail dress. If your cruise is more laid-back, the dress code may be even more relaxed, so check the specific guidelines for your ship.

Footwear is an important consideration. Comfortable walking shoes or sandals are a must for exploring ports, especially if you plan to wander through cobblestone streets or venture into nature trails. Pack slip-resistant footwear for onboard activities and excursions like zip-lining or hiking. Having a variety of shoes ensures you're ready for anything.

Sun protection is non-negotiable in the Caribbean. Bring a high-SPF sunscreen and reapply it often, especially after swimming. A reusable water bottle is also a smart addition to keep you hydrated throughout the day, both on the ship and during shore excursions. If you're prone to motion sickness, consider packing remedies like motion sickness bands or medication, even though modern ships are typically stable.

When it comes to planning, research is your best friend. Familiarize yourself with the ports on your itinerary and note the attractions or activities that interest you the most. Decide in advance whether you'll book excursions through the cruise line, go with local operators, or explore independently. Many excursions require advance reservations, so planning ahead can save you from missing out on popular experiences.

It's also worth preparing a small day bag for excursions. Include essentials like your cruise ID, cash or credit cards, a phone or camera, and any specific items for the day's activity, such as snorkeling gear or hiking maps. Pack snacks and reusable utensils for longer outings, and keep a small first-aid kit handy for minor mishaps.

Travel documents are another priority. Make sure your passport is valid for at least six months beyond your return date, as some countries have strict entry requirements. Check if any of your destinations require visas or special documentation. Having digital and printed copies of your itinerary, tickets, and emergency contacts ensures you're well-prepared for any situation.

Remember to pack with versatility in mind. A lightweight jacket or sweater can be useful for cooler evenings or air-conditioned spaces on the ship. Bring a small laundry kit if you plan to reuse items, as well as a waterproof bag to keep your electronics safe during beach or water excursions.

The goal of packing and planning is to create a balance where you feel prepared without being overwhelmed by luggage. Thoughtful preparation will give you the freedom to fully immerse yourself in the Caribbean experience, soaking in every colorful sunset, flavorful dish, and unforgettable moment.

Best Times to Cruise

The best time to visit Caribbean cruise ports depends on what you're seeking from your trip. Each season brings its own charm, shaping the atmosphere, experiences, and opportunities across these vibrant islands. With warm temperatures year-round, the Caribbean is an alluring destination in every season, but understanding the nuances of each can help you make the most of your journey.

Spring in the Caribbean feels like a fresh breeze after the cooler months, with temperatures ranging from the mid-70s to mid-80s Fahrenheit. The islands bloom with life, making it an excellent time to enjoy outdoor adventures and explore the natural beauty. Beaches are less crowded, allowing for tranquil moments by turquoise waters. This is also a great time for snorkeling and diving, as the seas tend to be calm and visibility high. Bring lightweight clothing and sunscreen, as the sun can be strong, but evenings may call for a light jacket, especially if you plan to dine outdoors by the water.

One of spring's highlights is the abundance of cultural festivals, like the vibrant Easter and Carnival celebrations in islands such as St. Lucia and Trinidad. These events showcase the Caribbean's rich heritage through music, dance, and colorful parades. To fully enjoy these festivities, plan accommodations and tickets early, as they are highly anticipated by locals and visitors alike. Prices in spring are moderate, offering a balance between affordability and favorable weather. Compared to the busier winter months, you'll find more room to explore while still benefiting from excellent travel conditions.

Summer in the Caribbean offers its own unique allure, with temperatures rising slightly into the mid-80s to low 90s Fahrenheit. The season is characterized by lush, green landscapes following the spring rains, creating picturesque settings for hiking and exploring. Though summer marks the beginning of hurricane season, storms are less common early in the season, and most itineraries include ports with reliable weather. Pack for heat and humidity, with breathable fabrics, a reusable water bottle, and plenty of sun protection.

Summer is an ideal time for families, as school vacations bring more travelers to the islands. Beaches and attractions can be lively, creating a vibrant, festive atmosphere. Water sports are particularly popular, from jet skiing and paddleboarding to sailing along the coastline. For those interested in local events, festivals like Antigua's Carnival in July and August celebrate Caribbean culture with infectious energy. However, the increased crowds mean higher prices for cruises and excursions. Booking early can secure better rates and ensure availability at popular attractions. Summer's dynamic energy makes it a fantastic choice for social travelers who enjoy bustling environments.

Autumn brings a quieter side to the Caribbean as the peak summer crowds recede. Temperatures remain warm, ranging from the high 70s to low 90s, but the pace of life slows, creating a relaxed and peaceful ambiance. This is the height of hurricane season, so travelers should stay informed about weather forecasts and consider travel insurance. The benefit of visiting during this time is the opportunity to experience the Caribbean with fewer tourists, often at significantly lower costs. Pack versatile clothing and a lightweight rain jacket, as brief tropical showers are common.

Autumn is perfect for those who prefer a more intimate travel experience, with uncrowded beaches and serene evenings. It's also a time when local flavors come to life, as harvest festivals like the Barbados Food and Rum Festival showcase the region's culinary excellence. Travelers should plan for flexibility, as some excursions may adjust to accommodate weather changes. While autumn doesn't offer the same level of guaranteed sunshine as other seasons, its charm lies in its tranquility and affordability.

Winter is the Caribbean's most popular season, drawing travelers seeking an escape from colder climates. Temperatures are comfortably warm, usually in the 70s and 80s, with dry, sunny days that are ideal for exploring both land and sea. This season showcases the islands at their most vibrant, with bustling markets, lively beach bars, and perfect conditions for sailing and snorkeling. Pack for mild warmth, with plenty of swimwear and casual attire for daytime adventures, as well as dressier options for evenings on board or in port towns.

Winter is also when the Caribbean hosts some of its most celebrated events, such as Junkanoo in the Bahamas and Christmas festivals across the islands. The demand for cruises and accommodations is at its peak, so booking well in advance is crucial to secure your desired itinerary. Prices are higher during this period, reflecting its popularity, and ports can be crowded. However, the festive atmosphere and near-perfect weather make it a favorite time to visit for good reason.

Each season in the Caribbean offers a distinct perspective on its beauty and culture. Spring and autumn appeal to those seeking balance and quieter moments, while summer's vibrancy and winter's festive charm cater to travelers who thrive in lively settings. By considering your personal preferences and goals, you can choose the season that best aligns with your vision for a perfect Caribbean escape.

Duration of your trip

The duration of your trip plays a significant role in shaping your Caribbean cruise experience. Whether you're planning a short getaway or a longer exploration of the region, the length of your trip will influence everything from the number of destinations you visit to the pace of your adventure. Choosing the right duration depends on your interests, schedule, and what you hope to get out of the journey.

For a quick escape, a three- to five-day cruise can be ideal. These shorter itineraries typically focus on a few highlights, giving you a taste of the Caribbean without requiring a long commitment. They are perfect for first-time cruisers or those looking to squeeze a little sunshine and relaxation into a busy schedule. You might visit popular ports like Nassau in the Bahamas or Cozumel in Mexico, offering just enough time to explore the beaches, indulge in local cuisine, and enjoy some water activities. While brief, these trips can be wonderfully refreshing, offering a compact but memorable adventure.

If you have more time, a seven- to ten-day cruise allows for a deeper dive into the Caribbean. With a week or more, you can experience a variety of islands, each with its unique charm. This duration often includes stops at some of the larger islands, such as Jamaica or the Dominican Republic, alongside smaller, less-crowded gems like St. Kitts or Antigua. These trips strike a great balance between relaxation and exploration, giving you time to enjoy both the onboard amenities and the rich cultural and natural offerings of the ports. You can savor the diversity of the region, from vibrant local markets to lush rainforests and coral reefs.

For those who want a truly immersive experience, consider cruises lasting two weeks or longer. These itineraries often explore both the Eastern and Western Caribbean, or even extend to include parts of South America. A longer trip allows you to delve into the history, traditions, and landscapes of a broader range of destinations. Imagine strolling through colonial streets in San Juan, Puerto Rico, hiking in the green hills of St. Lucia, and discovering the underwater wonders of Bonaire, all in one trip. These extended cruises are perfect for those who value depth and variety, offering the chance to fully unwind and engage with the beauty of the Caribbean.

When planning the duration of your trip, think about the pace that suits you best. If you enjoy a leisurely approach, allowing for long days at sea to relax and recharge, a longer cruise might be your style. If you prefer to pack your days with activities and see as much as possible, even a shorter trip can feel fulfilling with well-chosen excursions. Consider the time of year, too—seasonal weather patterns and events might influence how long you want to spend in the region.

It's also worth noting how trip length affects your packing and preparation. Shorter cruises require lighter packing, while longer journeys might call for more variety in clothing and essentials. Planning ahead ensures that your time aboard and ashore is as enjoyable and stress-free as possible.

The best duration for your trip is the one that aligns with your goals and interests. Whether it's a whirlwind escape or a leisurely voyage, the Caribbean offers something for every traveler. With the right balance of time and planning, your trip will leave you with a treasure trove of memories and experiences to cherish long after you've returned home.

Caribbean Cruise a budget

Exploring a Caribbean cruise port on a budget is entirely possible, and you can still enjoy all the vibrant experiences this tropical paradise has to offer. With a little planning and some insider knowledge, you can have an amazing time without breaking the bank. Here's a comprehensive guide to help you make the most of your budget while maintaining comfort and enjoyment.

Timing your visit is one of the most important factors in maximizing savings. The Caribbean sees a drop in prices during the shoulder seasons, typically in late spring and fall. This is when the crowds are fewer, and the prices for excursions and accommodations are lower. Visiting during these times not only helps keep costs down but also allows for a more relaxed and personal experience. You'll find that many attractions and restaurants aren't as crowded, so you can truly soak in the atmosphere without feeling rushed or overwhelmed. On the other hand, the high season, particularly around Christmas and New Year's, can lead to higher prices, so if you want to stick to a budget, it's best to avoid these peak periods.

When it comes to accommodations, there are several affordable options that still offer comfort and a great location. Many cruise ports have hostels or guesthouses where you can enjoy a clean, safe, and budget-friendly place to rest after a day of exploring. For example, in Nassau, you can find hostels that charge as little as $30 to $50 a night. These are great for those who are looking for a no-frills, economical stay. Vacation rentals are also an excellent option for travelers on a budget, offering you the freedom to cook your meals and potentially save on dining out. Platforms like Airbnb and Vrbo offer a range of affordable properties that allow you to experience the local culture in a more personal way. Prices for vacation rentals vary depending on the location, but you can often find charming apartments or houses for around $70 to $100 per night.

Activity planning on a budget doesn't mean sacrificing quality experiences. Many Caribbean ports have a wealth of free or low-cost activities that are just as enjoyable as pricier tours. Exploring the local culture and natural beauty is a great way to start. In many destinations, you can enjoy a leisurely walk around colorful markets or historical districts for free. For example, in Old San Juan, Puerto Rico, you can wander through cobblestone streets, visit the historic forts (such as Castillo San Felipe del Morro, which has an affordable entrance fee), and enjoy the architecture without spending much at all. If you're into nature, there are plenty of public beaches where you can spend the day sunbathing and swimming at no cost. In some locations, like Grand Turk, you can also find hiking trails or nature reserves that require no entry fee.

For dining on a budget, the Caribbean offers a fantastic selection of local food that won't cost a fortune. Street food is a great way to experience authentic flavors at a fraction of the price of restaurant meals. Many Caribbean ports have food trucks or small stalls selling delicious snacks like jerk chicken, empanadas, or fresh seafood. In places like Jamaica or Trinidad, you can enjoy a hearty meal for just a few dollars. If you prefer to eat like a local, head to neighborhood eateries that serve traditional dishes at lower prices than tourist-focused restaurants. Markets are also great for picking up fresh fruits or snacks to enjoy on a picnic at the beach. For example, in St. Lucia, you can grab some tropical fruits or local pastries from the Castries Market for a light and affordable lunch.

Transportation is another area where you can save money. Instead of booking pricey excursions through your cruise line, consider using local buses or shared taxis to get around. Public transportation is often much cheaper and can be a fun way to see a different side of the destination. In some places, like Barbados or St. Thomas, local buses run along popular routes for just a few dollars. You can also look into buying day passes for buses or trains in certain destinations, which can save you money if you plan to do a lot of sightseeing. If you're staying in a guesthouse or vacation rental, ask the owner for transportation recommendations or even arrange for a local guide who can show you the best budget-friendly spots.

There are always additional ways to save while visiting a Caribbean cruise port. Many destinations offer discount cards or passes that give you access to multiple attractions for one low price. These cards often include entry to museums, parks, and other cultural sites, and can save you a significant amount if you plan on visiting several attractions. It's also worth doing a bit of research on free or discounted days for certain attractions, as many places offer special deals during the off-season or certain times of the week.

Visiting a Caribbean cruise port on a budget is completely doable, and it can be just as rewarding as a more expensive trip. By timing your visit right, choosing affordable accommodations, exploring free or low-cost activities, and enjoying local food and transportation options, you can have a memorable and enjoyable experience without overspending. Remember, the best experiences often come from immersing yourself in the local culture and natural beauty, both of which are abundant in the Caribbean, no matter your budget.

Choosing the right Cruise Line

Choosing the right cruise line for your journey to a Caribbean cruise port can greatly influence your overall experience. With various cruise options available, each catering to different preferences and travel goals, selecting the right one can be a key part of planning a memorable trip. Here's a comprehensive guide to help you find the best cruise line for your Caribbean adventure.

When it comes to cruise lines, there are four main types to consider: mainstream, luxury, premium, and budget. Mainstream cruise lines, such as Royal Caribbean and Carnival, are known for their variety of activities and amenities that cater to families and groups. These cruises often feature entertainment options like Broadway-style shows, water parks, and family-oriented excursions. Luxury cruise lines like Regent Seven Seas and Crystal Cruises offer an all-inclusive experience with fine dining, spacious suites, and personalized service. These are perfect for those seeking a high-end experience with a focus on comfort and exclusivity. Premium lines like Norwegian Cruise Line provide a balance of luxury and affordability, offering relaxed dining options, stylish accommodations, and a mix of activities for all ages. Budget-friendly options, such as MSC Cruises and Princess Cruises, focus on providing great value without sacrificing comfort. These cruises are ideal for travelers who want a quality experience at an affordable price.

For a trip to a Caribbean cruise port, several well-known cruise lines offer unforgettable itineraries. Royal Caribbean, known for its large ships and extensive activities, is perfect for families or groups. Their ships feature rock climbing walls, ice skating rinks, and even surf simulators, making it an excellent choice for those looking for adventure. A typical Royal Caribbean cruise to the Caribbean lasts around 7 to 9 days, with prices starting at about $500 per person for an interior cabin. Norwegian Cruise Line offers a range of itineraries with a more relaxed atmosphere, including their popular "Freestyle Cruising" option, where guests can dine when and where they want. Norwegian's cruises range from 5 to 10 days, with prices starting around $350 per person. Luxury options like Regent Seven Seas or Crystal Cruises are perfect for those looking to indulge in elegance. A 7-day cruise with these lines can cost from $3,000 per person, but it includes all meals, drinks, excursions, and tips, which means no surprise fees onboard.

The type of cruise line that works best for you depends on your travel style and goals. Families will find that mainstream lines like Carnival or Royal Caribbean provide ample activities to keep everyone entertained, from kids' clubs to family excursions. These cruises are also known for their flexibility, offering early-boarding and dining times to accommodate families with young children. For couples or honeymooners looking for relaxation and romance, luxury cruise lines or premium options like Celebrity Cruises and Norwegian's Haven suites provide an adult-only experience with a quieter, more sophisticated atmosphere. If you're a solo traveler or part of a group of friends, cruise lines that offer a mix of social activities and cultural immersion, such as Holland America Line, could be a great fit. These lines offer enriching shore excursions that allow you to explore local history and culture in a way that suits your interests.

Seasonal considerations can also affect your choice of cruise line. High season in the Caribbean is typically during the winter months (December to April), which brings more crowds and higher prices, especially on luxury lines. To get better rates, you can consider traveling during the shoulder season, which falls between May and early June or September through November. During these times, you'll find fewer crowds and more affordable prices, with many lines offering promotions or discounts. Keep in mind that the weather is generally warm year-round in the Caribbean, but hurricane season from June to November may bring some risks, so it's important to check the weather forecast when booking your trip.

Local insights can also provide valuable information on which cruise lines excel at providing authentic Caribbean experiences. According to seasoned travelers and local experts, smaller cruise lines like Windstar Cruises or Azamara offer intimate itineraries that can take you to lesser-known islands, giving you a chance to experience the Caribbean's hidden gems. These lines often focus on more personalized experiences, including visits to off-the-beaten-path ports and smaller island communities, which can be a refreshing alternative to the mainstream destinations.

When booking your cruise, there are several tips to help ensure you find the best deal. First, it's important to shop around and compare prices across different cruise lines, websites, and travel agencies. Many cruise lines offer early-booking discounts, group rates, or promotions for certain dates, so be sure to look out for these deals. If you're flexible with your travel dates, you may be able to find last-minute offers or price reductions. Websites like CruiseCritic and Kayak allow you to check multiple options at once, helping you make an informed decision. It's also worth considering booking directly with the cruise line, as they may offer exclusive deals or onboard credits that third-party agents might not provide.

Personalization and flexibility are crucial elements of many modern cruise experiences. For instance, many cruise lines allow you to customize your trip with additional excursions, spa packages, or specialty dining experiences. If you're a foodie, you might want to book a culinary experience or a wine tasting onboard. For those who want a more adventurous experience, booking excursions like zip-lining, scuba diving, or hiking can make your trip even more memorable. Cruise lines such as Royal Caribbean and Norwegian also offer flexible itineraries that allow you to mix and match ports of call, so you can create a tailored experience that suits your preferences.

Choosing the right cruise line for your Caribbean journey involves considering your personal preferences, travel goals, and budget. Whether you're looking for adventure, luxury, or cultural immersion, there's a cruise line that can meet your needs. By doing thorough research, being flexible with your dates, and booking early, you can find the perfect cruise line for your ideal Caribbean experience.

Entry and visa requirements

When planning a Caribbean cruise, it's essential to understand the entry and visa requirements for the countries you'll be visiting. These requirements can vary depending on your nationality, the countries you're traveling to, and the type of cruise you've booked. Below is a comprehensive guide to help travelers navigate visa requirements and the application process for a smooth entry into Caribbean destinations.

To determine if you need a visa for the Caribbean, start by researching the specific countries you'll be visiting on your cruise. Some Caribbean nations, such as the Bahamas, Jamaica, the Dominican Republic, and Barbados, have lenient entry requirements for travelers from certain countries, especially for those arriving by cruise. For example, travelers from the United States, Canada, the European Union, and several other countries do not typically require a visa for short stays, often just needing a valid passport. However, other Caribbean nations might require visas depending on your nationality, the length of your stay, or the purpose of your visit. It's important to check visa requirements well in advance of your trip, as each country has different rules. In some cases, travelers may be able to enter with a visa waiver or a pre-arranged tourist visa. Additionally, some destinations are part of the Schengen Area, which allows travelers with a valid Schengen visa to visit multiple countries with one visa. If you are traveling to several countries in the Caribbean that have signed the Schengen Agreement, you may be able to use this visa to enter.

The visa application process for Caribbean destinations varies from country to country, but there are common steps travelers can follow to ensure a smooth experience. Start by checking the visa requirements for each country you will visit, as this will help you determine whether you need a visa at all. Many Caribbean nations provide detailed visa information on their official immigration websites, including the documents required and how to apply. For those who do need a visa, the process generally begins with filling out an application form online or in person at the relevant consulate. You will likely need to provide a range of documents, such as a valid passport (with at least six months' validity from your arrival date), a copy of your travel itinerary (showing your flight and cruise bookings), proof of accommodation for the duration of your stay, and evidence of sufficient funds to cover your expenses. In some cases, you may also need to submit a recent passport-sized photo and pay a visa processing fee. If applying for a Schengen visa for multiple Caribbean countries, make sure to apply at the embassy of the country you will visit first or stay the longest.

Practical tips for a smooth visa application process include starting early. Visa processing times can vary, so it's best to apply well in advance of your cruise departure date to avoid any last-minute issues. Make sure all your documentation is complete, as incomplete or incorrect applications can lead to delays or rejections. It's also a good idea to use official government resources to verify visa requirements, rather than relying on third-party websites, which may offer outdated or inaccurate information. If you're unsure about the visa application process or have specific questions, contact the consulate or embassy for the most accurate and up-to-date information.

To help readers understand the process better, consider using a checklist or flowchart that outlines the steps involved in applying for a visa to Caribbean countries. This can include steps like: checking the specific country's visa requirements, gathering the necessary documents (passport, itinerary, etc.), submitting the application online or in person, attending an interview (if required), paying the visa fee, and waiting for approval. A checklist can be an easy-to-follow guide, ensuring travelers don't miss any critical steps. Additionally, offering sample scenarios can illustrate how the process might differ for various nationalities. For example, a U.S. citizen traveling to the Bahamas may only need a valid passport and no visa, while a traveler from India may need to apply for a tourist visa to visit multiple Caribbean nations. These examples can provide clarity on how the process varies depending on the traveler's country of origin.

By being prepared and staying informed about the visa requirements for the Caribbean countries you'll be visiting, you can ensure a hassle-free experience when embarking on your cruise. Make sure to verify all the necessary documentation and start the application process early to avoid stress as your trip approaches. Whether you're traveling for relaxation, adventure, or cultural exploration, understanding entry requirements will help you focus on enjoying your cruise rather than worrying about visa details.

CHAPTER 2.
GETTING TO CARIBBEAN CRUISE DEPARTURE POINT

Caribbean Cruise departure point : Arrival and Orientation

Arriving at the Caribbean cruise departure point can feel like the start of an exciting adventure. Whether you're flying into a bustling international airport or a smaller, more relaxed one, the journey begins as soon as you land. Each cruise departure point has its own vibe, but the process is generally straightforward, allowing you to transition smoothly from the airport to the cruise terminal.

As you step off the plane, the first thing you'll notice is the warm, tropical air. Caribbean airports are often located near the coast, so you might catch a glimpse of the sparkling blue waters as you walk through the terminal. Depending on where you're flying into, the airport could be a large hub like Miami International Airport or a smaller regional airport like San Juan's Luis Muñoz Marín International Airport. Either way, the process is designed to get you to your cruise as quickly and smoothly as possible.

Once you've disembarked, your first stop will likely be customs and immigration. If you're flying internationally, you'll go through passport control, where an agent will check your travel documents and ask you a few questions about your trip.

It's always a good idea to have your passport ready and any forms that were required for entry. The process is usually quick, but it can take a bit longer during peak travel times. After you clear customs, you'll head to baggage claim to pick up your luggage, if it wasn't already checked directly to your cruise terminal. If your bags are already tagged for the cruise terminal, this step can be a little faster, and you can skip heading to baggage claim altogether.

After collecting your luggage or confirming it's been sent to the terminal, the next step is to make your way to the cruise port. Many Caribbean airports offer convenient shuttle services or taxis that take travelers directly to the cruise terminal. These shuttles are often well-marked and easy to find, and they're designed to handle large groups of cruisers. If you've arranged for a private transfer or are using a ride-sharing service, you'll find pick-up spots clearly marked outside the terminal. For those who are more independent, public transportation options or rental car services are available, though this can take a bit longer and may require some additional planning.

As you make your way to the port, you'll get your first taste of the local atmosphere. The streets around the cruise terminal are often bustling with activity, with people coming and going from their vacations, local vendors selling souvenirs, and tourists excited for their Caribbean adventures. It's a good time to take in the scenery, stretch your legs, and enjoy the excitement of getting closer to your cruise.

Upon arrival at the cruise terminal, there are usually clear signs directing you to check-in areas. The terminal will be designed for efficiency, with lines for each cruise line or group of passengers based on your ship. The check-in process involves presenting your cruise documents, such as your booking confirmation and passport, and having your security photo taken. You'll also be given your cruise card, which serves as your room key and payment method for onboard purchases. Once you've checked in, there may be a waiting area before you board the ship. During this time, feel free to relax, grab a snack, or browse through the nearby shops while you wait for the official boarding process to begin.

If this is your first cruise, the orientation process at the cruise terminal can feel like a whirlwind, but it's very straightforward. Port agents are available to answer any questions you have, and they're used to dealing with travelers who might be a little unsure about the process. Don't hesitate to ask for help if you need directions or assistance with any part of your journey. Most terminals are equipped with comfortable seating, Wi-Fi access, and amenities like restrooms and cafes to make your wait as comfortable as possible.

When it's time to board, you'll be directed to the gangway where you'll officially step onto the ship. This is the moment when your vacation truly begins, as you walk into the grand entrance of the cruise ship, greeted by crew members and the excitement of being on board. Depending on the time of day and the number of passengers, the boarding process can take anywhere from 30 minutes to an hour, but it moves quickly and efficiently.

Arriving at a Caribbean cruise departure airport and getting to your ship is a simple process. The airports and terminals are designed with cruisers in mind, making the experience relatively smooth and stress-free. It's always a good idea to arrive a little earlier than planned, just in case of any unexpected delays or long lines. With everything taken care of, you can relax and enjoy the first steps of your Caribbean adventure. From the airport to the ship, the journey is part of the excitement, and soon enough, you'll be setting sail toward your next destination.

Journey to Caribbean Cruise Departure points

The journey from the airport to the cruise departure point is the first step in your Caribbean adventure, and planning it well can set the tone for the rest of your trip. There are several transportation options to consider, each with its benefits, depending on your preferences, budget, and timing.

Taxis are a convenient choice for those seeking a direct and hassle-free ride. At airports like Miami International or Orlando International, taxis are readily available outside baggage claim. The fare to PortMiami averages around $30 to $40 and takes about 20 to 30 minutes, depending on traffic. From Orlando to Port Canaveral, the trip is longer—about 45 minutes to an hour—with taxi fares ranging from $100 to $150. While taxis are more expensive than some alternatives, they provide the advantage of door-to-door service.

Rideshare options like Uber and Lyft have gained popularity for their reliability and often lower cost compared to traditional taxis. In Miami, rideshare fares to the cruise port typically range from $15 to $25. In San Juan, Puerto Rico, rideshare services are limited, but local taxi apps or pre-arranged private car services can fill the gap. Booking your ride in advance through the app ensures you have a vehicle waiting, especially during peak travel times.

Shuttle services are a cost-effective way to transfer from the airport to the cruise port. Many shuttle companies operate in major cruise departure cities. For instance, at Port Canaveral, shared shuttles are available for as low as $30 per person one way. Cruise lines often offer their own shuttle services that can be booked during your cruise reservation process. These services typically cost around $20 to $30 per person and offer peace of mind as they are timed to align with ship embarkation schedules. However, cruise line shuttles may involve waiting for other passengers and may not be as flexible as private options.

Public transportation can be the most affordable option, though it requires more time and planning. In Miami, the Miami-Dade Transit system connects the airport to downtown Miami via the Metrorail, from where you can take a taxi or rideshare to the cruise port. While economical, public transit may not be ideal for those with extensive luggage or limited time.

If you have mobility challenges, many transportation services offer accessible vehicles. In Miami and Orlando, for example, taxis and rideshares with wheelchair accessibility are available. It's a good idea to notify your chosen service of your requirements in advance to ensure a suitable vehicle is dispatched.

Travelers should allow extra time for transfers, especially in cities known for heavy traffic like Miami. Aim to arrive at the cruise port at least two hours before your scheduled boarding time to avoid any last-minute stress. Keep an eye on real-time traffic updates and plan your journey accordingly. Managing luggage is another key factor; many rideshares and taxis can accommodate standard suitcases, but larger groups may require a vehicle with additional capacity.

One of the highlights of your transfer journey can be the scenic views or unique local experiences along the way. Driving from Orlando to Port Canaveral offers glimpses of Florida's natural landscapes and the Kennedy Space Center in the distance. In San Juan, the drive from Luis Muñoz Marín International Airport to the cruise port takes you through vibrant neighborhoods where you might catch a glimpse of colorful murals or bustling street vendors.The trip from the airport to your cruise departure point can be seamless and enjoyable with proper Planning, setting the stage for the Caribbean escape that lies ahead.

CHAPTER 3.
EASTERN CARIBBEAN PORTS

Nassau, Bahamas

Nassau, Bahamas, is a vibrant and welcoming destination that draws thousands of cruise passengers each year. Situated on New Providence Island, it is the capital city of the Bahamas and one of the most popular ports of call in the Caribbean. Known for its stunning beaches, rich history, and vibrant cultural scene, Nassau offers an array of experiences that appeal to all types of travelers.

Geographically, Nassau is located just 185 miles off the coast of Florida, making it an easy getaway for those embarking on a Caribbean cruise. The city's tropical climate means warm temperatures year-round, and its colorful colonial architecture and scenic waterfront make it a visually striking place. Nassau's unique blend of cultures—stemming from African, European, and Caribbean influences—adds a layer of depth and charm that visitors can experience through its music, food, and art.

Nassau's cultural and historical significance is evident in every corner of the city. The island was originally inhabited by the Lucayan Taíno people before becoming a key location for European colonization. Over the centuries, it has played a crucial role in the slave trade, piracy, and colonial rule. Nassau was famously the home of notorious pirate Edward Teach, better known as Blackbeard, and the city's history is forever linked to the Age of Sail. The influence of the British Empire is still visible in Nassau's architecture, and visitors can explore remnants of colonial rule at the many forts, churches, and old buildings throughout the city. Today, Nassau stands as a cultural melting pot, with its mix of African, British, and Bahamian heritage offering a fascinating glimpse into the island's complex past.

When you arrive in Nassau, there is no shortage of things to see and do. Some of the most popular attractions include the Queen's Staircase, a historic landmark built by slaves in the late 18th century that leads to the Fort Fincastle. The fort, built in 1793, offers panoramic views of the city and the harbor. Another must-visit spot is the Nassau Straw Market, where visitors can find handcrafted Bahamian goods like straw hats, bags, and jewelry. For those interested in art, the National Art Gallery of the Bahamas provides a deep dive into the island's contemporary and historical art scene. History buffs will also want to visit the Pirates Museum, which offers an interactive look at Nassau's pirate past.

If you're looking for a more relaxed experience, Nassau has some of the Caribbean's most stunning beaches. Cable Beach, with its white sand and clear turquoise waters, is perfect for sunbathing, while Junkanoo Beach, located near the cruise port, is a great spot to unwind after a busy day of sightseeing. If you're up for adventure, you can swim with pigs at the Exuma Cays or dive into the blue hole for an unforgettable underwater experience.

When it comes to local cuisine, Nassau doesn't disappoint. Bahamian food is a unique fusion of Caribbean, African, and British influences. A local favorite is conch, a type of shellfish that can be served fried, in salads, or as chowder. Visitors should also try Bahama Mama, a cocktail made from rum, coconut, and fruit juices, which is a popular drink among locals and tourists alike. For a more traditional meal, head to the Fish Fry at Arawak Cay, a popular spot among locals for fresh seafood served in casual, beachside eateries. If you're in the mood for something sweet, try a slice of guava duff, a traditional Bahamian dessert made with guava and served with a butter rum sauce.

For cruise passengers visiting Nassau, the port is located just a short distance from the city center, making it convenient to explore on foot. When you disembark from your ship, you'll be greeted by a variety of transportation options, including taxis, buses, and water taxis that can take you to nearby destinations. If you prefer a more organized experience, several companies offer guided tours that will take you to Nassau's top attractions, often including transportation.

In terms of accessibility, Nassau is fairly well-equipped to handle travelers with disabilities. Many of the main tourist attractions, including the Queen's Staircase and Fort Fincastle, have accessible entrances, and several beaches in Nassau offer wheelchair rentals. However, it's recommended to check with your cruise line or tour provider in advance to confirm accessibility details.

The best times to visit Nassau are during the off-peak seasons, which run from late spring to early fall. During this time, you'll find fewer crowds and more affordable prices, making it a great time to enjoy the city's attractions without the usual rush. However, keep in mind that Nassau can be quite warm year-round, so visitors should dress lightly, wear sunscreen, and stay hydrated.

While Nassau is known for its popular tourist spots, there are also hidden gems worth exploring. Venture off the beaten path to discover the island's charming local markets, colorful neighborhoods, and smaller cultural sites that often get overlooked. For a truly unique experience, visit the island's native gardens or take a boat tour to the nearby islands for a more tranquil, less commercialized experience of the Bahamas.

Nassau is a place where history, culture, and natural beauty blend together seamlessly. Whether you're interested in exploring its historical sites, enjoying its vibrant culture, or simply relaxing on one of its beautiful beaches, Nassau has something to offer every traveler. By taking the time to explore the city's rich heritage and its lesser-known spots, you can make the most of your time in this exciting and diverse Caribbean destination.

Philipsburg, St. Maarten

Philipsburg, located on the Dutch side of the island of Saint Martin (Sint Maarten), is a vibrant and bustling port that serves as a prime destination for cruise passengers in the Caribbean. Known for its breathtaking beaches, dynamic shopping scene, and lively atmosphere, Philipsburg draws visitors with its unique blend of cultures, offering a window into both Dutch and French influences on the island. The town's location on the picturesque Great Bay provides travelers with stunning views of the turquoise waters and surrounding hills, making it a strikingly beautiful port of call.

Geographically, Philipsburg sits on the southern coast of Saint Martin, the Caribbean island shared by the Netherlands and France. This strategic location made Philipsburg an important port historically, serving as a hub for trade and commerce. The town itself is compact but packed with history, and the local ambiance is a melting pot of Caribbean traditions, European colonial influences, and a laid-back island vibe. This blend makes it a culturally rich and diverse destination where visitors can experience a variety of activities, from lounging on pristine beaches to exploring its colorful history.

Philipsburg's cultural and historical significance is deeply intertwined with the colonial history of Saint Martin. The island has switched hands between French and Dutch control multiple times over the centuries, and Philipsburg was founded by the Dutch in 1763. This historical backdrop has shaped the town's character, from the architectural style of its buildings to the local customs and cuisine. Philipsburg's role as a major port city has also contributed to its multiculturalism, attracting settlers, traders, and pirates in its early days. The town is named after the Dutch governor at the time, Philipsburg, and is still very much alive with a sense of its maritime past.

When it comes to attractions and activities, Philipsburg is a treasure trove of experiences. One of the most popular places to visit is Front Street, the town's main thoroughfare, which offers a mix of duty-free shops, local boutiques, restaurants, and cafes. The street is often bustling with tourists looking to pick up souvenirs, including jewelry, watches, and local arts and crafts. For those interested in history, the Sint Maarten National Museum located on Front Street offers a glimpse into the island's rich past, with exhibits about its early inhabitants, colonial history, and the development of the port.

Beaches in Philipsburg are among the best in the Caribbean, and Great Bay Beach is one of the most famous. With its long stretch of soft sand and calm, clear waters, it's perfect for swimming, lounging, or enjoying a drink at one of the beachfront bars. For a more secluded experience, visitors can take a short trip to Little Bay Beach, which is quieter and known for its crystal-clear waters, ideal for snorkeling and water sports. Philipsburg is also the gateway to a variety of boat excursions, including sailing trips, snorkeling tours, and dolphin watching, allowing visitors to experience the island from the water.

Philipsburg offers an exciting mix of dining options that reflect the island's blend of Caribbean, Dutch, and French culinary traditions. Local restaurants serve a variety of delicious dishes, with seafood being the main highlight. Conch fritters, a popular Bahamian dish made from conch meat, are a must-try in Philipsburg. Fresh fish such as snapper, mahi-mahi, and tuna are often served grilled or in flavorful Caribbean stews. For those looking for a true local experience, the island's food markets offer an opportunity to sample local fruits, vegetables, and street food. A number of beachfront restaurants offer casual yet delicious dining, with some featuring live music and stunning views of the bay.

When cruising into Philipsburg, ships dock at the Port of Philipsburg, which is conveniently located near the center of town. The port's location makes it easy for visitors to walk directly into the town and start exploring. From the dock, the beach is just a short walk away, and Front Street is easily accessible for those looking to shop or grab a bite to eat. The port is equipped with various services and amenities to cater to tourists, including shops, restrooms, and information desks.

Getting around Philipsburg is relatively easy. Taxis are plentiful, and they can take you to nearby beaches or other points of interest around the island. However, for those who prefer a more adventurous mode of transportation, bicycles and scooters are available for rent. The town is small enough to explore on foot, and many of its main attractions are within walking distance of each other. For visitors who want to venture further, public buses and water taxis are available for exploring other parts of the island, including the French side of Saint Martin.

The operating hours for most attractions in Philipsburg are generally from 9:00 AM to 5:00 PM, although this may vary depending on the season and the specific venue. During the high season, from December to April, the town sees an influx of tourists, so it's a great time to explore, though expect more crowds. The low season, from May to November, offers a quieter experience but also comes with the possibility of rain or hurricanes, so it's important to check the weather forecast before planning outdoor activities.

The best time to visit Philipsburg is during the cooler months, from November to April. The weather is more pleasant, and there are fewer chances of rain. It's also during this period that the island hosts its most popular events, such as the annual Carnival, held in April, which is a vibrant celebration of music, dance, and local traditions. While this is the high season for tourism, it is the best time to experience the full energy of Philipsburg and the island at large.

As with any popular tourist destination, travelers should exercise caution. While Philipsburg is generally safe, visitors should be mindful of their belongings and avoid walking around with large sums of cash or valuables, especially in crowded areas. It's also advisable to stick to well-lit areas at night and to take taxis when venturing further out of the town center. For those with mobility issues, the town is fairly accessible, with many attractions offering ramps and accessible entrances. However, some beaches and excursions may be more difficult to navigate, so it's recommended to check accessibility in advance when booking activities.

Beyond the usual tourist destinations, Philipsburg offers some hidden gems worth exploring. A short walk or drive from the main town will take you to the peaceful and scenic Maho Beach, famous for its close proximity to Princess Juliana International Airport, where you can watch planes fly just above the beach. For a quieter and more cultural experience, head to the quaint village of Oyster Pond on the French side of the island, where you can enjoy a more relaxed, authentic Caribbean atmosphere.

Philipsburg, with its perfect blend of history, culture, shopping, beaches, and local cuisine, provides a rich experience for any traveler. The town offers a wonderful balance of sightseeing, relaxation, and adventure, making it a must-visit stop on any Caribbean cruise. Whether you're looking to explore the island's past, sample its diverse cuisine, or simply soak up the sun on its beautiful beaches, Philipsburg has something to offer everyone.

San Juan, Puerto Rico

San Juan, Puerto Rico, is a vibrant, historic port city and one of the most popular destinations for cruise passengers in the Caribbean. Situated on the northern coast of the island, San Juan serves as the capital of Puerto Rico and is a blend of old-world charm and modern urbanity. With its picturesque beaches, colorful colonial architecture, and rich cultural heritage, San Juan offers travelers a multifaceted experience. Geographically, it's positioned on a natural harbor, which made it an important port for centuries, and today it continues to serve as a key entry point to Puerto Rico, making it a gateway to the island's diverse landscapes and rich traditions.

The city's cultural diversity stems from its deep Spanish roots, combined with African, Taino, and American influences. As the oldest colonial city under the U.S. flag, San Juan offers a fascinating mix of European and Caribbean cultures, with colonial buildings sitting alongside modern skyscrapers. The city is also a UNESCO World Heritage site, with its fortified walls and streets that have witnessed over 500 years of history. San Juan's culture is reflected in its lively festivals, music, art, and cuisine, which have evolved over time to create a unique blend of island and Latin American influences.

San Juan's historical significance is immense. It was founded in 1521 by the Spanish, making it one of the oldest European-established cities in the Americas. The city's strategic location on the Caribbean allowed it to play a key role in trade and defense during the colonial period. San Juan is home to some of the most historically significant sites in the Americas, including Castillo San Felipe del Morro, a 16th-century fort that has guarded the city for centuries, and the ancient city walls that still surround Old San Juan. This historical backdrop makes San Juan an integral part of Puerto Rico's identity, as it has witnessed major events in the island's evolution, from Spanish colonial rule to its current status as a U.S. territory.

Key attractions and activities in San Juan offer a deep dive into both its historical past and lively present. A must-see is Old San Juan, with its cobblestone streets, brightly colored Spanish colonial buildings, and historic forts like El Morro and Castillo San Cristóbal. Visitors can take a walking tour of the district, exploring the many plazas, churches, and the famous El Paseo del Morro, a promenade with sweeping views of the sea. The vibrant street art scene in Old San Juan also stands out, with murals and galleries showcasing Puerto Rican talent.

For those interested in the natural beauty of San Juan, the beaches are a major attraction. Condado Beach and Isla Verde Beach are both easily accessible from the city center and offer opportunities for swimming, sunbathing, and water sports. Travelers looking for a more serene experience can visit the nearby El Yunque National Forest, a lush rainforest located just an hour's drive from the city. Hiking trails, waterfalls, and the island's endemic flora and fauna await nature lovers.

San Juan is also home to an exciting culinary scene, with a mix of traditional Puerto Rican dishes and contemporary twists on Caribbean cuisine. The island's cuisine is known for its bold flavors and heavy use of local ingredients like plantains, rice, beans, seafood, and pork. Mofongo, a dish made from mashed plantains and often served with shrimp, chicken, or pork, is a must-try, along with lechón (roast pork) and pasteles (a type of tamale). The city has a variety of dining options, from casual street food vendors to upscale restaurants. La Placita de Santurce is a local hotspot for trying traditional dishes and enjoying the lively atmosphere. For more formal dining, try restaurants like Marmalade or José Enrique, which offer innovative takes on Puerto Rican flavors.

Cruise ships typically dock at the Pan American Pier or the Old San Juan Cruise Terminal, both of which are conveniently located near the heart of the city. From the terminal, it's a short walk to Old San Juan, where most of the major attractions are situated. The proximity to key sights makes it easy for passengers to explore the city on foot or take short taxi rides to nearby areas. Shuttle services are also available for tourists who want to visit more distant attractions like El Yunque or the beaches.

Getting around San Juan is relatively easy, with a number of transportation options available. Taxis are plentiful and can take visitors to most major attractions, but be sure to confirm the fare before starting the ride. Public buses are another affordable way to get around, though they may not always be as convenient or timely as taxis. The city also has a convenient hop-on, hop-off trolley service in Old San Juan, which is a great way to see the main sights without the hassle of walking. If you're feeling adventurous, consider renting a bike or scooter to explore the city at your own pace.

When planning a visit to San Juan, it's important to be mindful of the local weather, which can be hot and humid year-round. The peak tourist season is from December to April, when the weather is cooler and drier, making it the best time to explore the city and its surrounding areas. However, this also means more crowds and higher prices. The off-season, from May to November, is less crowded but can be hot and rainy, and it coincides with hurricane season, so it's important to keep an eye on weather forecasts during this time.

Safety is generally not a concern for tourists in San Juan, but like in any city, it's important to stay alert, especially in less busy areas or after dark. Avoid carrying large amounts of cash, and be cautious of pickpockets, particularly in crowded areas or on public transportation. The beaches near Old San Juan are safe, but as with all tourist destinations, it's best to keep an eye on your belongings and avoid leaving them unattended. San Juan is fairly accessible, with many hotels, restaurants, and attractions offering wheelchair access. However, some older parts of Old San Juan have cobblestone streets and may not be as accessible for travelers with mobility issues.

While the major attractions in San Juan are well-known, there are also hidden gems that offer a deeper look at Puerto Rican life and culture. Consider visiting the Santurce neighborhood, where you'll find vibrant street art, local galleries, and the lively Mercado de Santurce, a market that showcases the island's agricultural products. For a peaceful retreat, head to the Jardín Botánico, the Botanical Garden of San Juan, which offers a serene environment with a variety of tropical plants. The Museo de Arte de Puerto Rico is another gem for art lovers, with an impressive collection of Puerto Rican art spanning centuries.

In conclusion, San Juan offers cruise passengers a rich tapestry of cultural, historical, and natural experiences. Whether you're strolling through the colorful streets of Old San Juan, sampling Puerto Rican cuisine, or exploring the island's beaches and rainforests, there's something for everyone in this dynamic city. The perfect mix of colonial charm, vibrant culture, and scenic beauty makes San Juan a destination worth exploring, and it encourages travelers to step beyond the typical tourist path to uncover the many layers of its history and identity.

St. Thomas, U.S. Virgin Islands

St. Thomas, U.S. Virgin Islands, is a captivating destination for cruise passengers, offering a perfect blend of natural beauty, rich history, and vibrant culture. Located in the Caribbean Sea, St. Thomas is part of the U.S. Virgin Islands and serves as the gateway to the archipelago. The island is known for its stunning beaches, crystal-clear waters, and mountainous terrain, making it a paradise for outdoor enthusiasts and relaxation seekers alike. St. Thomas is also one of the busiest cruise ports in the Caribbean, drawing visitors from around the world to experience its warm hospitality and unique Caribbean charm.

Geographically, St. Thomas is the most developed of the U.S. Virgin Islands, with its capital, Charlotte Amalie, being a central hub for commerce and tourism. The island's geographical location made it an important stop for trade and military defense throughout history, and today, it continues to be a major tourist destination. Its close proximity to neighboring islands, including St. John and St. Croix, makes St. Thomas a convenient starting point for exploring the U.S. Virgin Islands and the surrounding Caribbean.

St. Thomas has a fascinating cultural and historical background that deeply influences the island's identity. Originally inhabited by the Taino people, the island was later colonized by the Danish in the 17th century. St. Thomas was an important port for the Danish West India and Guinea Company, dealing in sugar, rum, and slaves. The island became part of the U.S. Virgin Islands in 1917, when the United States purchased the territory from Denmark. The rich colonial history, combined with the influence of African, Caribbean, and European cultures, has shaped St. Thomas into a culturally diverse and vibrant community. Events like the Carnival, celebrated every spring, showcase the island's African, European, and indigenous heritage through music, dance, and food.

St. Thomas offers an array of attractions and activities that cater to all types of travelers. The island's crown jewel is its beaches, with Magens Bay being the most famous. Known for its calm, turquoise waters and soft sand, Magens Bay is a perfect spot for swimming, sunbathing, or enjoying a beachside picnic. For those interested in water sports, St. Thomas offers excellent snorkeling, scuba diving, and sailing opportunities. The coral reefs around the island are teeming with marine life, including colorful fish, sea turtles, and rays.

Many excursions offer boat trips to nearby smaller islands or uninhabited cays, where visitors can enjoy secluded beaches and pristine waters.

Charlotte Amalie, the capital of St. Thomas, is a historic port town with a bustling harbor and picturesque streets. The town is named after a Danish queen, and its colonial architecture and charming cobblestone streets transport visitors to a bygone era. Popular attractions in Charlotte Amalie include Fort Christian, the oldest standing structure in the U.S. Virgin Islands, and Blackbeard's Castle, a historic landmark linked to pirate lore. For shopping enthusiasts, Charlotte Amalie is home to duty-free shops, where visitors can purchase jewelry, perfumes, and local handicrafts. The island also offers scenic views from the Skyline Drive, where visitors can take in panoramic vistas of the island, harbor, and nearby cays.

Beyond the beaches and historical sites, St. Thomas also offers cultural experiences, such as visiting the Virgin Islands Heritage Museum, which highlights the island's past, and the National Park at Coral Bay, which preserves the island's natural beauty. Local festivals and events, such as the St. Thomas Carnival, provide an exciting chance to experience the island's lively music, food, and traditions.

The local cuisine of St. Thomas is a flavorful fusion of Caribbean, African, and European influences. Seafood is abundant, and dishes like conch fritters, whelk stew, and grilled snapper are popular among locals and visitors alike. One dish that should not be missed is "saltfish and fungi," a traditional meal made of salted cod and a cornmeal dumpling.

For a sweet treat, try the island's famous "guavaberry rum," a drink made from native guava berries and rum, or indulge in coconut-based desserts such as "coconut tarts" or "coconut candy."

There are numerous dining options on the island, ranging from casual beachside eateries to upscale restaurants. For authentic local food, try the Gladys' Café in Charlotte Amalie, a beloved spot for Caribbean staples, or the All-American Grill, known for its laid-back atmosphere and tasty dishes. For a more elegant experience, visit the 5-star French restaurant, the Bleu at The Ritz-Carlton, offering gourmet dishes and stunning ocean views. If you're in the mood for a drink, head to one of the island's rum bars to enjoy the local spirits.

Cruise ships dock at the Crown Bay Dock or the West Indian Company Dock in Charlotte Amalie, both of which are close to the heart of the city's attractions. The Crown Bay Dock is just a short taxi ride or shuttle away from Magens Bay and the historic district. The West Indian Company Dock is right in the center of Charlotte Amalie, making it easy to walk to shops, restaurants, and historical sites. From both docks, visitors can easily access taxis or shuttle buses to explore the island.

Transportation on St. Thomas is easy to navigate, with taxis being the most common way for tourists to get around. Most taxis operate on a flat-rate system, which makes it easy to know the cost before you travel. While public transportation is available, it's not as widely used by tourists, so taxis or rented vehicles are often the most convenient options. Many hotels and tour operators offer shuttle services to major attractions, and there are also ferry services to nearby St. John and Tortola, British Virgin Islands. If you're interested in exploring the island independently, renting a car is an option, though driving on the left side of the road may take some getting used to for those accustomed to right-hand driving.

The best time to visit St. Thomas is from December to April, when the weather is sunny and the island enjoys its dry season. This period is also the most popular time for cruise passengers, so expect more crowds at major tourist sites. For a more relaxed experience, consider visiting during the off-season (May to November), although this coincides with the rainy season and potential hurricanes. Despite the rain, the island remains a warm and welcoming destination year-round.

St. Thomas is generally a safe destination for travelers, but like any popular tourist location, visitors should exercise caution. Be mindful of your personal belongings, especially in crowded areas or while shopping, as pickpocketing can occur. It's also advisable to avoid traveling alone in remote areas after dark. As with many Caribbean islands, it's a good idea to carry some local currency (U.S. dollars) as small vendors may not always accept credit cards.

For travelers with disabilities, many attractions in St. Thomas are wheelchair accessible, including Fort Christian and parts of the historical district. However, some of the natural attractions, such as hiking trails and beaches, may be more challenging to navigate. It's always best to check in advance about accessibility options if you have specific needs.

For hidden gems and local insights, take a trip to the less-visited parts of St. Thomas, like the remote Coki Beach, which is perfect for snorkeling and offers a quieter atmosphere than the more famous Magens Bay. Visit the St. Thomas Synagogue, the second-oldest synagogue in the Western Hemisphere, for a unique glimpse into the island's Jewish heritage. For those interested in nature, the Virgin Islands National Park, just a short ferry ride away on St. John, is a great option for hiking, wildlife watching, and exploring unspoiled beaches.

St. Thomas offers an enriching experience for cruise passengers, blending history, culture, and natural beauty. From its historic landmarks to its pristine beaches and vibrant culinary scene, the island has something for everyone. While the main attractions are undoubtedly captivating, there's a wealth of hidden gems and unique experiences waiting for those who venture off the beaten path. Whether you're a history buff, nature lover, or foodie, St. Thomas is a destination that promises to leave a lasting impression.

CHAPTER 4.
WESTERN CARIBBEAN PORTS

Galveston, Texas

Galveston, Texas, is a charming and historically rich port city on the Gulf Coast, offering a perfect blend of coastal beauty, cultural heritage, and exciting activities for cruise passengers. Located about 50 miles southeast of Houston, Galveston is one of the largest cruise ports in the United States, drawing visitors with its captivating mix of beaches, historical landmarks, and vibrant local culture. The city's strategic location along the Gulf of Mexico has made it an important hub for maritime trade and tourism, contributing to its diverse character and significance as a cruise destination.

The attractions and activities in Galveston provide something for everyone. Beach lovers will enjoy the city's extensive coastline, with popular spots like Stewart Beach and Galveston Island State Park offering opportunities for swimming and sunbathing. Visitors can also engage in watersports such as kayaking and fishing. For a more laid-back experience, the Galveston Island Historic Pleasure Pier provides a nostalgic amusement park atmosphere with classic rides and food stands.

Galveston's historical sites are among its most well-known attractions. The Moody Mansion offers a glimpse into the life of wealthy families who once lived in the city. The Galveston Island Historic District features Victorian-era homes and tree-lined streets perfect for leisurely strolls or guided tours. The historic Strand District, lined with shops and restaurants, showcases Galveston's maritime past.

The city's seafaring history is showcased at the Galveston Naval Museum, housing the USS Cavalla submarine and USS Stewart destroyer escort. History buffs will appreciate the Texas Seaport Museum, which highlights Galveston's role as a key port during the 1800s. Another fascinating attraction is the Bishop's Palace, an architectural gem that reflects Galveston's opulent past.

For nature enthusiasts, Galveston Island State Park offers hiking trails and bird watching opportunities to explore coastal ecosystems. Nearby, the Galveston Bay Foundation provides guided eco-tours to learn about local habitats and wildlife.

Galveston boasts a vibrant arts and culture scene. Throughout the year, visitors can enjoy live music, festivals, and events such as Mardi Gras Galveston and Dickens on the Strand festival celebrating its Victorian past.

Food is another highlight of visiting Galveston. Known for its delicious seafood, local restaurants serve fresh catches from the Gulf. Classic dishes include shrimp gumbo and fried catfish. For a true taste of Galveston's coastal cuisine, head to Gaido's Seafood Restaurant or The Spot beachside bar.

Cruise ships dock at two main locations in Galveston: the Port of Galveston includes both the Texas Cruise Terminal and Galveston Cruise Terminal. Both are conveniently located close to the city center, allowing easy access to shops and attractions. The Port of Galveston is well-equipped to handle large cruise ships and offers ample parking for passengers who choose to drive.

Getting around Galveston is simple with various transportation options available including taxis, rideshare services like Uber and Lyft, rental cars, and a free trolley service that runs along key areas of the city. For those looking to explore at their own pace, biking is popular with several shops offering rentals.

Galveston's major attractions are generally open year-round; however, some seasonal variations may affect availability. The summer months are peak tourist season; for a more relaxed experience, consider visiting during fall or spring when crowds are thinner.

When visiting Galveston, it's essential to keep safety tips in mind. While generally safe for tourists, being aware of your surroundings is advisable. Also be cautious on beaches due to potential rip currents; use sunscreen to protect against intense Texas sun exposure.

For visitors with disabilities, many major attractions are wheelchair accessible including Moody Gardens and Historic Pleasure Pier. It's recommended to contact local attractions in advance for specific accommodations.

Local insights can be found by exploring beyond main tourist areas; one hidden gem is the Galveston Island Ferry offering free rides across to Bolivar Peninsula with spectacular views of the Gulf Coast. Moody Gardens features interactive exhibits perfect for family-friendly experiences.

Galveston offers an incredible mix of history, culture, and natural beauty—making it an ideal port for cruise passengers to explore. From historic landmarks and beaches to delicious seafood and lively events, there's something for everyone in this memorable destination that invites you back time after time.

Cozumel, Mexico

Cozumel, Mexico, is one of the most popular cruise destinations in the Caribbean, known for its stunning beaches, vibrant marine life, and rich cultural heritage. Situated off the eastern coast of the Yucatán Peninsula, Cozumel is the largest island in Mexico's Caribbean, and it is famous for being a gateway to both natural beauty and ancient Mayan history. The island is a prime destination for divers, beach lovers, and history enthusiasts alike, offering everything from crystal-clear waters to archaeological sites, making it a must-see stop for cruise passengers.

Cozumel's historical and cultural significance is deeply intertwined with its ancient Mayan heritage. The island was considered a sacred place by the Mayans, who revered the goddess Ix Chel, the goddess of fertility and love, and built several structures in her honor. The island has been inhabited for thousands of years, with evidence of Mayan settlements dating back to at least the 1st century AD. Today, the island is a mix of modern Mexican culture and ancient traditions, with its history evident in both the ruins and local customs.

For cruise passengers, Cozumel offers a range of attractions and activities that cater to a variety of interests. One of the most famous attractions is the island's remarkable coral reefs, which are part of the Mesoamerican Reef System, the second-largest barrier reef in the world. This makes Cozumel a world-class destination for snorkeling and scuba diving. The clear waters and abundant marine life, including colorful fish, sea turtles, and even dolphins, offer an unforgettable experience. Popular dive sites include Palancar Reef, Colombia Reef, and Devil's Throat, all of which are accessible by boat from the island.

Beyond the ocean, Cozumel is also known for its natural beauty. For those interested in nature and wildlife, the Punta Sur Eco Park is a must-see. This protected reserve is home to diverse ecosystems, including mangroves, wetlands, and jungles, as well as the island's most beautiful beaches. Visitors can explore the park by walking, cycling, or even kayaking through its lagoons. Punta Sur is also home to the Celarain Lighthouse, which offers panoramic views of the island and the Caribbean Sea.

For history lovers, the San Gervasio Ruins are a must-visit. This ancient Mayan site, located in the heart of the island, was once a significant pilgrimage center dedicated to the goddess

Ix Chel. The site is well-preserved and offers a glimpse into the island's role in Mayan culture. Other historical sites worth exploring include the Cozumel Museum, which showcases the island's history from its Mayan roots to its modern-day role as a major tourist destination.

In addition to its historical and natural attractions, Cozumel is also home to a vibrant cultural scene. The island hosts various festivals throughout the year, such as the Carnival of Cozumel, a colorful celebration filled with parades, music, and dancing. This event, held in the days leading up to Lent, is one of the most important cultural celebrations on the island. The island also boasts a thriving art scene, with local galleries displaying works by Mexican artists, as well as traditional crafts such as handmade jewelry and textiles.

For dining, Cozumel offers a delicious array of local Mexican cuisine, with an emphasis on fresh seafood. One of the most popular dishes is "Ceviche," a refreshing mix of raw fish, lime juice, onions, and cilantro, perfect for the island's tropical climate. Another must-try dish is "Cochinita Pibil," a slow-cooked pork dish infused with achiote and citrus, a regional specialty. For an unforgettable dining experience, head to "La Choza" for traditional Mexican flavors in a cozy, authentic setting. Another excellent option is "Rolandi's," offering a mix of Italian and Mexican cuisine with an incredible view of the Caribbean.

Cruise ships dock at the main pier in Cozumel, which is located just a few miles from downtown San Miguel, the island's primary town. The dock area is very well-equipped, with shops, restaurants, and even an art gallery, offering visitors a chance to shop for local crafts or enjoy a quick meal before heading out to explore the island. Many cruise passengers choose to explore San Miguel itself, which is filled with colorful buildings, local markets, and vibrant shops selling souvenirs, clothing, and artisanal goods. For those looking for more adventure, various tour operators offer excursions that take visitors to the island's more remote areas, such as the eco-park or secluded beaches.

Getting around Cozumel is relatively easy, as the island is small and compact. Taxis are readily available and can be flagged down at the pier or booked in advance. For those wishing to explore more independently, rental scooters and cars are also an option. Biking is another popular way to explore the island, with many shops offering bike rentals. Cozumel is a pedestrian-friendly destination, especially in the town of San Miguel, where many attractions are within walking distance.

As for operating hours, most attractions in Cozumel are open daily, though it's important to note that many close in the early evening, typically around 5 or 6 PM. It's also worth noting that certain attractions, like the San Gervasio Ruins, can be more crowded during peak cruise season (from December to April), so visiting early in the day can help avoid crowds. Likewise, the weather can be a factor to consider, as Cozumel has a tropical climate, with the rainy season running from May to October. The best time to visit Cozumel is during the cooler, dry months of November through April.

When visiting Cozumel, it's important to take a few safety precautions. While the island is generally safe for tourists, petty crime, such as pickpocketing, can occur in crowded areas. It's advisable to keep an eye on your belongings, especially in busy markets or when on the beach. Additionally, while Cozumel is known for its friendly locals, it's a good idea to avoid isolated areas after dark. For beachgoers, it's important to be aware of water conditions and any posted warnings about rip currents.

Cozumel is also a very accessible destination, with most of the major attractions offering wheelchair access. Many taxis are equipped for disabled travelers, and most public areas in San Miguel are accessible to those with mobility challenges.

To truly experience Cozumel beyond the usual tourist paths, visitors should consider taking a trip to the less-visited north side of the island. Here, you can find secluded beaches, quiet lagoons, and untouched nature. Another hidden gem is the Cozumel Pearl Farm, where visitors can learn about pearl cultivation and take a guided tour of the farm's remote location.

Cozumel, Mexico, offers a rich mix of history, culture, and natural beauty, making it an ideal stop for cruise passengers seeking adventure, relaxation, or cultural exploration. Whether you're diving in the crystal-clear waters, wandering through ancient Mayan ruins, or savoring local Mexican delicacies, Cozumel provides a diverse and memorable experience that will leave you with lasting memories of this beautiful island.

Costa Maya, Mexico

Costa Maya, located on the eastern coast of the Yucatán Peninsula in Mexico, is a growing cruise port that has gained immense popularity due to its unique blend of natural beauty, ancient history, and cultural experiences. Positioned on the Caribbean Sea, Costa Maya is part of the state of Quintana Roo and serves as a gateway to the region's rich Mayan heritage, tropical beaches, and exciting adventures. The port's relative proximity to iconic destinations like Tulum, Chichen Itza, and the second-largest barrier reef in the world makes it a standout stop for cruise passengers.

Costa Maya's geographical significance is primarily rooted in its location along the Caribbean coastline, a region known for its lush jungles, pristine beaches, and the Mesoamerican Reef. This area is one of the world's most biodiverse marine ecosystems, drawing divers, snorkelers, and nature lovers. The town of Mahahual, which is a short distance from the cruise terminal, has seen rapid development in recent years, transitioning from a small fishing village into a bustling tourist hub. Despite its development, Costa Maya has managed to maintain a laid-back, less commercialized atmosphere compared to other major ports in the region, making it an appealing alternative for travelers seeking a more relaxed vibe.

Key attractions and activities in Costa Maya include both natural and cultural experiences that will leave visitors with lasting memories. The beaches here are the perfect retreat for sunbathers and swimmers. Mahahual, just a short distance from the port, is home to a beautiful beach where visitors can relax on soft sand and enjoy the gentle waves of the Caribbean Sea. Many beach clubs offer day passes with amenities such as sunbeds, food, and drinks, along with opportunities for water sports like kayaking and paddleboarding.

For those interested in nature and wildlife, Costa Maya offers some of the best snorkeling and diving experiences in the Caribbean. The Mesoamerican Reef, located just offshore, is teeming with marine life, including vibrant coral formations, tropical fish, sea turtles, and even nurse sharks. Several tour operators in the area offer snorkeling and diving trips to the reef, as well as opportunities to swim with dolphins at the nearby dolphinarium. For a truly unique experience, visitors can also take part in boat tours that offer the chance to explore nearby mangrove forests and lagoon systems.

History enthusiasts will find plenty to explore in Costa Maya as well. The nearby Chacchoben Ruins are a well-preserved Mayan archaeological site that offers visitors a chance to explore ancient pyramids, temples, and plazas that were once the center of Mayan life. The site is relatively quiet compared to other famous ruins like Chichen Itza, making it an ideal spot for those looking for a more peaceful and intimate experience with history. For those interested in more remote sites, Kohunlich, another Mayan city, is home to impressive stelae and a collection of well-preserved buildings. These ruins are nestled in the jungle, offering a sense of discovery and adventure.

For local cuisine, Costa Maya offers authentic Mexican and Yucatán dishes, with fresh seafood playing a central role in many meals. Visitors should try "Tikin Xic," a traditional Yucatán dish made from fish marinated in achiote, citrus juices, and herbs before being grilled. "Ceviche" is another popular dish, made from fresh fish or shrimp cured in lime juice and mixed with cilantro, onions, and chilies. For a more casual experience, local food stands in Mahahual offer tacos, quesadillas, and grilled corn. The restaurants around the port area also serve a wide range of Mexican specialties, such as tamales and mole, giving visitors a chance to dive into the region's culinary delights.

Costa Maya's cruise ship docking facilities are located at the port of the same name, which is a self-contained destination with shops, restaurants, and entertainment options. It is located just a short walk or shuttle ride away from Mahahual, where the majority of local restaurants, shops, and attractions are located. Many visitors choose to book excursions directly through their cruise line, which typically includes transportation to the main attractions, such as the Chacchoben ruins, the beaches, and other nature reserves.

Transportation options for getting around Costa Maya are diverse. Taxis are readily available at the port and are a convenient way to get to the nearby beaches or other attractions. For those looking to explore more independently, bicycle rentals are popular, especially for short trips to Mahahual or local eco-parks. Another option is to rent a scooter or golf cart, which provides a fun and easy way to explore the area at your own pace. Shuttle services between the port and various destinations, such as the ruins or beach clubs, are often available through local tour operators and are a convenient option for those wishing to avoid negotiating taxi fares.

Operating hours for most of Costa Maya's attractions are generally from 8 AM to 5 PM, though they may vary depending on the season or specific attraction. The best time to visit Costa Maya is during the cooler months, from December to April, when the weather is more comfortable and rain is less likely. The port can get busy during peak cruise season, so it's a good idea to plan excursions early in the day to avoid crowds. Keep in mind that the weather in Costa Maya is tropical, so visitors should be prepared for warm temperatures year-round and bring sunscreen, water, and light clothing for comfort.

As with any travel destination, it's important to keep a few safety tips in mind while in Costa Maya. The region is generally safe for tourists, but petty theft can occur, especially in crowded areas. Travelers should be cautious with their belongings, avoid leaving valuables unattended at the beach, and stick to well-lit areas at night. While the area is friendly, it's advisable to book excursions and transportation through reputable companies to ensure a smooth and secure experience.

Costa Maya is also a great destination for travelers with disabilities. Many of the attractions, such as the beach clubs and the port facilities, are wheelchair accessible, and taxis are available that can accommodate wheelchairs or other mobility devices. It's always a good idea to contact tour operators or local businesses ahead of time to confirm that specific facilities can meet accessibility needs.

For those seeking to experience a more authentic side of Costa Maya, exploring beyond the usual tourist destinations is highly recommended. The town of Mahahual offers a more laid-back experience compared to the bustling cruise port, with its local markets, quiet beaches, and community-driven atmosphere. Additionally, a visit to the nearby village of Xcalak, located about an hour away, provides a glimpse into rural Mexican life and offers opportunities for eco-tourism, such as bird watching and nature walks.

Costa Maya, Mexico, offers a rich tapestry of experiences that highlight the region's natural beauty, history, and culture. Whether you're lounging on the beach, diving in the crystal-clear waters of the Mesoamerican Reef, or exploring ancient Mayan ruins, Costa Maya promises a memorable and diverse experience for cruise passengers. The combination of relaxing activities and cultural exploration makes Costa Maya an ideal stop for anyone looking to connect with the heart of the Yucatán Peninsula.

Grand Cayman, Cayman Islands

Grand Cayman, the largest of the three Cayman Islands, is a tropical paradise in the Caribbean Sea that draws travelers for its stunning beaches, clear waters, and unique blend of British colonial heritage and Caribbean charm. Located south of Cuba and to the northwest of Jamaica, it is the financial and tourism hub of the Cayman Islands. Grand Cayman is an idyllic destination for cruise passengers, offering a variety of attractions, from natural wonders and wildlife to a rich cultural history.

Grand Cayman has a fascinating history that intertwines indigenous cultures, colonial influences, and modern-day prosperity. The island was first discovered by Christopher Columbus in 1503, although it was initially avoided by European explorers due to its hostile waters and treacherous reefs. In the 17th century, the island was settled by the British, who used it as a base for pirates and traders. Today, the Cayman Islands remain a British Overseas Territory, and the island's culture reflects a fusion of British, Jamaican, and other Caribbean influences.

Key attractions and activities in Grand Cayman provide a wide variety of experiences that appeal to all types of travelers. For those who enjoy the sea, the island offers world-class snorkeling and diving opportunities. The Stingray City Sandbar is one of Grand Cayman's most iconic attractions. Just off the coast, visitors can interact with friendly stingrays in shallow, crystal-clear water—a once-in-a-lifetime experience. Additionally, the nearby reefs around the island, including the famous Bloody Bay Wall, are popular spots for divers, offering vibrant coral formations and a wealth of marine life.

For a more laid-back experience, visitors can head to Seven Mile Beach, widely regarded as one of the best beaches in the world. The beach offers pristine white sand and calm waters, ideal for swimming, lounging, or enjoying water sports like paddleboarding and kayaking. For nature lovers, the island has several natural parks and reserves, such as the Queen Elizabeth II Botanic Park, where visitors can admire local flora and the rare blue iguana, an endangered species native to the island.

History buffs will also appreciate Grand Cayman's historical sites, such as the Cayman Islands National Museum, located in George Town, where visitors can learn about the island's past, from its pirate days to its role as a global financial center. Another historical site of note is Pedro St. James, a restored plantation house that played a key role in the island's fight for independence.

When it comes to dining, Grand Cayman offers a diverse array of options that showcase the island's Caribbean flavors and international influences. Local dishes to try include conch fritters, Cayman-style lobster, and jerk chicken. Seafood lovers will find plenty of restaurants offering fresh, locally caught fish and seafood, often prepared with spices and tropical ingredients that give the dishes their distinctive flavors. Restaurants like The Wharf, located by the water, and The Cayman Islands Brewery offer both casual and fine dining experiences, with stunning views of the Caribbean Sea. The district of George Town is also home to several vibrant food markets, where visitors can try local snacks and freshly made dishes.

Cruise ships dock at the Port of George Town, which is conveniently located near many of the island's main attractions, including the central shopping area and several dining options. The port's proximity to George Town makes it easy for visitors to explore the island's shops, cafes, and local attractions without needing to travel far. From the port, it's a short walk or taxi ride to many of the island's best-known destinations, including Seven Mile Beach and the Cayman Islands National Museum.

Transportation options on Grand Cayman are varied and convenient. Taxis are readily available at the port and can take visitors to popular destinations such as the beaches, Stingray City, or the shopping areas in George Town. For those looking to explore independently, rental cars and scooters are available, though driving on the left side of the road is something to keep in mind. There are also local buses and shuttle services that provide affordable ways to travel around the island.

Most attractions in Grand Cayman are open year-round, though some may have adjusted hours during the off-peak season, which runs from May to November. The best time to visit is during the dry season, from December to April, when the weather is warm and sunny, and the island experiences fewer rain showers. This is also when the island sees the most tourists, so visitors should plan to arrive early to avoid crowds at popular attractions.

Safety in Grand Cayman is generally not a concern for most travelers. The island is known for being peaceful, with low crime rates. However, like any popular tourist destination, it's wise to keep personal belongings secure, especially on crowded beaches or in busy areas like George Town. While the island is quite safe, it's recommended to avoid isolated areas at night, especially if you're unfamiliar with the surroundings.

For travelers with disabilities, Grand Cayman is fairly accessible. The port and many of the island's main attractions have wheelchair-friendly facilities. Taxis and rental vehicles can be arranged to accommodate mobility needs, and public transportation in George Town is typically accessible. However, it's always a good idea to check in advance with specific tour operators or attractions to ensure that accommodations for disabilities are available.

Hidden gems in Grand Cayman include places like the Crystal Caves, located on the northern part of the island. These natural limestone caves are filled with beautiful stalactites and stalagmites and offer guided tours that explain the cave's history and geology. Another lesser-known attraction is the Cayman Turtle Centre, where visitors can learn about the island's conservation efforts for sea turtles, and even swim with them in a large lagoon.

Grand Cayman offers a diverse and enriching experience for cruise passengers, with something for everyone, from sun-seekers and divers to history enthusiasts and food lovers. The island's unique combination of natural beauty, cultural heritage, and modern amenities makes it an ideal destination for those looking to explore both the scenic and the historical sides of the Caribbean. With its welcoming atmosphere and wealth of experiences, Grand Cayman promises an unforgettable stop on any cruise itinerary.

Belize City, Belize

Belize City, the largest city in Belize, is a bustling port that blends rich history, vibrant culture, and natural beauty, making it a fascinating stop for cruise passengers. Located on the Caribbean coast, this vibrant city is Belize's primary gateway for international visitors, and its unique blend of colonial architecture, Caribbean influences, and proximity to ancient Mayan ruins makes it a standout destination.

Historically, Belize City has been a key part of the country's development, starting as a small settlement founded by the British in the early 18th century. It was established as the capital of British Honduras (now Belize) and was the primary point of entry for British settlers, traders, and enslaved Africans. The city has seen the rise and fall of several colonial empires and was even devastated by hurricanes, particularly Hurricane Hattie in 1961, which led to the relocation of the country's capital to Belmopan. However, Belize City remains the cultural and commercial heart of Belize, offering visitors a look at both the country's colonial past and its modern-day identity.

Key attractions and activities in Belize City offer a wide range of experiences, from exploring historical landmarks to enjoying the natural beauty that surrounds the city. One of the most popular excursions for cruise passengers is a visit to the Mayan ruins of Altun Ha, located just outside the city. Altun Ha is one of Belize's most famous archaeological sites, where visitors can explore ancient pyramids, temples, and plazas, learning about the powerful Mayan civilization that once thrived in the region. The site also features the Temple of the Sun God, home to one of the largest jade masks ever discovered.

For those looking to enjoy the coastal beauty, a visit to the nearby Belize Barrier Reef is a must. As the second-largest reef system in the world, it's a prime spot for snorkeling, scuba diving, and glass-bottom boat tours. The Hol Chan Marine Reserve and Shark Ray Alley, located off the coast of Ambergris Caye, are especially popular for seeing marine life up close, including nurse sharks, rays, and a variety of tropical fish.

Back in Belize City, the Belize City Museum offers an excellent introduction to the history of the city and the country. Housed in a former colonial prison, the museum's exhibits cover Belize's indigenous cultures, colonial history, and natural environment. Another historical landmark is St. John's Cathedral, a beautiful and historic church built in the 19th century with stunning stained-glass windows and colonial architecture.

For a taste of local culture, head to the bustling Albert Street, where visitors can shop for handmade crafts, local art, and souvenirs. The city's markets are vibrant and full of life, with a wide variety of fresh fruits, spices, and local goods. Belize City's harbor area is also home to the Fort Street Tourism Village, where cruise passengers can disembark and enjoy a selection of shops, restaurants, and bars.

Belize City's culinary scene reflects the diverse culture of the area, with an emphasis on fresh seafood, tropical fruits, and flavorful spices. Local dishes to try include rice and beans with stewed chicken, fry jacks (fried dough), and conch ceviche. The city is home to several great restaurants, including the smoky, lively Elvi's Kitchen, known for its traditional Belizean dishes and laid-back atmosphere. For a more contemporary dining experience, the Riverside Tavern offers a blend of Caribbean and international cuisine with views of the Belize River.

Cruise ships typically dock at the Fort Street Tourism Village, a commercial area that's just a short walk from the city center. From here, visitors can easily access the main attractions of Belize City, such as the Belize City Museum and the shops and markets along Albert Street. The port is a lively hub where you'll find taxis, shuttle buses, and tour operators ready to take you on guided excursions to nearby attractions.

Transportation options in Belize City are abundant. Taxis are the most common mode of transport for visitors, with fixed rates depending on your destination. Be sure to agree on the price before setting off to avoid misunderstandings. Local buses also run throughout the city, providing an affordable way to get around, though they may not be as comfortable or reliable as taxis. If you prefer to explore on your own, car rentals are available, though driving in Belize City can be challenging due to narrow streets and heavy traffic. Many visitors also take advantage of organized tours to the nearby Mayan ruins and marine reserves, which typically include transportation to and from the port.

Major attractions in Belize City typically operate from 8:00 AM to 5:00 PM, with some flexibility depending on the season. The best time to visit is during the dry season, from November to April, when the weather is sunny and warm. This is also the peak tourist season, so expect larger crowds at popular attractions. If you prefer a quieter experience, consider visiting during the off-season (May to October), though you may encounter more rain and humidity during these months.

Safety in Belize City is generally not a major concern for tourists, but it's always wise to take common-sense precautions. Stick to well-populated areas, especially in the evening, and be cautious with your belongings in crowded spaces. Petty theft, such as pickpocketing, can happen in tourist-heavy areas, so keep an eye on your valuables. Avoid wandering in unfamiliar or poorly lit areas at night.

Belize City is generally accessible for travelers with disabilities, with some attractions offering wheelchair-friendly access. However, it's recommended to check with specific tour operators and attractions beforehand to ensure they can accommodate your needs. Public transportation may not always be equipped for travelers with mobility challenges, so taxis or private tours are the best options.

Hidden gems in Belize City include a visit to the nearby Crooked Tree Wildlife Sanctuary, a peaceful nature reserve known for its birdwatching opportunities. This is an ideal destination for nature lovers seeking a quieter experience away from the crowds. Another lesser-known spot is the Government House, a beautiful colonial building that now serves as a museum. Though not often on the typical tourist itinerary, it provides great insights into Belize's colonial past.

In conclusion, Belize City offers a rich tapestry of experiences that showcase the country's vibrant culture, history, and natural beauty. From exploring ancient Mayan ruins to immersing yourself in the local food scene and enjoying the breathtaking marine life, Belize City is a destination that offers something for every type of traveler. Whether you're interested in history, adventure, or simply soaking up the laid-back atmosphere of the Caribbean, Belize City provides a perfect introduction to this stunning country. For cruise passengers, it's a destination that's not to be missed, offering an unforgettable blend of history, culture, and natural wonders.

Ocho Rios, Jamaica

Ocho Rios, Jamaica, is a scenic port town nestled on the northern coast of the island. The name "Ocho Rios" translates to "Eight Rivers" in Spanish, though the town is primarily known for its breathtaking beaches, waterfalls, and vibrant culture. Positioned along Jamaica's north coast, it's a popular stop for cruise ships due to its accessible location and the natural beauty surrounding it. Visitors are greeted by lush green hills, sparkling blue waters, and a variety of exciting attractions. The town's laid-back atmosphere, combined with its rich culture and history, makes it a must-visit destination on the island.

Culturally, Ocho Rios is a melting pot, influenced by indigenous, African, European, and Asian roots, which is reflected in its food, music, and lifestyle. This town is also famous for its role in Jamaica's tourism industry, attracting millions of cruise passengers each year. It was once a quiet fishing village but evolved into a major tourist hub after the opening of the Ocho Rios port, which continues to grow in popularity.

Historically, Ocho Rios has roots dating back to colonial Jamaica. During the 17th century, it was primarily a site for sugar production, and later it became a center for trade and commerce. The area gained further prominence when it became a major port for cruise ships in the 1980s. While Ocho Rios' modern-day appeal is largely due to its natural beauty and vibrant tourism scene, its heritage is embedded in the preservation of colonial-era architecture and the vibrant traditions that define Jamaican life today. The town is also known for being the filming location of the 007 James Bond movie *Dr. No*, adding another layer of global pop culture to its history.

For those visiting Ocho Rios, there's no shortage of must-see attractions. Dunn's River Falls is perhaps the most iconic site in the area. A stunning 600-foot waterfall, visitors can climb its tiers, swim in natural pools, or simply marvel at the view. For a more serene experience, the nearby Fern Gully offers a tranquil drive through a lush, fern-filled gorge, showcasing Jamaica's rich tropical vegetation. Another major draw is Dolphin Cove, where visitors can swim with dolphins, interact with stingrays, and explore the underwater world via glass-bottom boat tours.

A unique experience can be found at Mystic Mountain, where travelers can take a chairlift ride up the mountain, enjoy a bobsled ride through the rainforest, or zip-line over the canopy. This attraction combines thrilling activities with magnificent panoramic views of Ocho Rios and the Caribbean Sea.

For those interested in history, the Shaw Park Gardens offers a peaceful retreat, with beautiful flora and a small museum showcasing the island's colonial past. The town also offers several plantations and local homes open to visitors, allowing them to take a step back in time to learn about Jamaica's agricultural heritage.

When it comes to cuisine, Ocho Rios offers a diverse array of local Jamaican dishes. A visit to Jamaica wouldn't be complete without trying jerk chicken, a spicy, smoky dish made from marinated chicken grilled over pimento wood. Local eateries like Scotchies serve up authentic jerk food, while Island Grill offers more casual dining options. For seafood lovers, The Lobster Pot is a great spot to sample freshly caught seafood in a relaxed, seaside setting. If you're looking for something more upscale, the Couples Sans Souci resort offers a range of gourmet dining options with a view of the sea. For those craving something quick and sweet, try a Jamaican patty from a local bakery. These savory pastries are filled with spiced meat or vegetables and are a favorite street food across the island.

Cruise ships dock at the Ocho Rios Cruise Ship Terminal, located just outside the town center. From here, visitors can easily access local shops, markets, and attractions on foot. Most cruise passengers will find that the dock area is bustling with taxis, tour operators, and small cafes. Taxis are plentiful, and many drivers are eager to take visitors to nearby attractions like Dunn's River Falls or Mystic Mountain. For those wishing to explore on their own, renting a private vehicle is also an option, though driving on the left side of the road may require some getting used to.

Public transportation in Ocho Rios is available in the form of minibuses, though they can be less reliable compared to taxis. For a more authentic experience, visitors can also hop on a route taxi, a shared ride option that's often used by locals. However, taxis tend to be the easiest and safest option for tourists looking to get around the area. Many resorts and hotels also offer shuttle services to popular attractions, which can be a convenient option for cruise passengers who want to avoid the hassle of navigating the area themselves.

As for timing your visit, the best months to explore Ocho Rios are from November to mid-December and from January to April, when the weather is sunny and the chance of rain is minimal. The town can be crowded during the peak tourist season, especially around the holidays, so visiting early in the morning or later in the afternoon can help avoid the busiest crowds. If you're hoping for a quieter experience, consider visiting in the off-season, from May to October, though this comes with the possibility of rain.

When it comes to safety, Ocho Rios is generally safe for tourists, but as with any travel destination, there are some precautions to consider. Stick to well-lit areas at night and always use reputable taxi services or organized tours. In the busy market areas, be aware of your belongings and avoid engaging with aggressive street vendors.

Accessibility options in Ocho Rios are somewhat limited but improving. Many of the larger hotels and resorts offer accessible rooms and facilities, and some of the main attractions, such as Dunn's River Falls and Dolphin Cove, have made efforts to accommodate visitors with mobility challenges. However, certain sites, particularly those that require hiking or climbing, may present challenges for those with physical disabilities.

For travelers looking to dive deeper into the local culture, some lesser-known gems include the town's local art scene. The Ocho Rios Craft Market, located near the cruise terminal, is a great place to browse handcrafted jewelry, wood carvings, and paintings made by local artisans. Another hidden gem is the nearby Blue Hole, a secluded swimming spot that's less crowded than Dunn's River Falls but just as stunning. Surrounded by lush jungle and crystal-clear waters, it's a tranquil place for a refreshing swim.

Ocho Rios, Jamaica, offers cruise passengers an unforgettable experience that combines natural beauty, adventure, rich culture, and mouthwatering cuisine. From exploring iconic waterfalls and climbing mountains to savoring authentic jerk chicken and experiencing the island's lively atmosphere, Ocho Rios provides something for every type of traveler. Beyond the typical tourist attractions, the area's local art, hidden gems, and cultural experiences await those who wish to go deeper into Jamaican life. A visit to Ocho Rios is not just about the sights, but about embracing the island's vibrant soul and enjoying its warmth and hospitality.

Falmouth, Jamaica

Falmouth, Jamaica, located along the north coast of the island, is a vibrant port town that offers a perfect mix of rich history, natural beauty, and modern conveniences. Once a bustling sugar port, Falmouth has undergone significant development over the past decade, positioning itself as a prime cruise destination. Its proximity to other popular attractions such as Montego Bay, Ocho Rios, and Negril makes it an ideal stop for cruise passengers exploring Jamaica's northern coast. With its charming colonial architecture, beautiful beaches, and rich cultural heritage, Falmouth has carved out a niche as a vibrant gateway to Jamaica's history and natural wonders.

Culturally, Falmouth is a blend of African, European, and Jamaican influences. The town has roots dating back to the late 1700s, when it was established as a bustling port for the sugar industry. Over the years, it has retained much of its historic charm, with buildings dating back to the 19th century. Today, Falmouth remains an important cultural hub, known for its unique fusion of old and new, where colonial-era buildings sit side by side with modern developments aimed at the tourism industry.

One of the major highlights of visiting Falmouth is the town's rich blend of historical and modern attractions. The Falmouth Heritage Walk provides visitors with a guided tour through the heart of the town, showcasing its colonial architecture, including the Georgian-style courthouse and the St. Peter's Anglican Church, which dates back to the 18th century. The Falmouth Port is another notable site, where visitors can enjoy the sight of ships docked against the backdrop of the town's unique skyline.

For those who enjoy natural beauty, Falmouth offers some of the most scenic and pristine beaches on the island. The nearby Burwood Beach is a great spot for swimming and lounging in the sun, while the James Bond Beach, just outside of town, offers an opportunity to explore the picturesque coastline made famous by the 007 movie franchise. In addition to its beaches, Falmouth is near the stunning Martha Brae River, where visitors can enjoy a relaxing rafting trip down the river, guided by locals who provide both a peaceful and scenic experience.

If you're seeking more adventure, head to the nearby Luminous Lagoon, one of Jamaica's most unique natural phenomena. This lagoon glows at night due to the presence of microscopic organisms that emit a blue light when disturbed, creating a mesmerizing glow. A boat tour of the lagoon at night is a must-see activity for any visitor to Falmouth.

When it comes to food, Falmouth offers a delightful array of local Jamaican dishes that reflect the island's diverse culinary heritage. Traditional favorites like jerk chicken and jerk pork can be found at local street vendors and restaurants throughout the town. For a true taste of Jamaica, try a plate of escovitch fish, a tangy and spicy fried fish dish that is a staple in Jamaican cuisine. Travelers can also sample other dishes such as curry goat, ackee and saltfish, or the popular Jamaican patty—a savory pastry filled with spiced meat.

One of the best places to sample authentic Jamaican food is at the Culinary Arts Center, located near the cruise terminal. Here, visitors can taste freshly prepared dishes and interact with chefs who share their insights into Jamaican cooking techniques. For a more casual dining experience, the nearby Water Square offers several restaurants and snack bars that serve both local and international fare.

Cruise ships dock directly at the Falmouth Cruise Port, which is just a short walk from the town center. The port area is modern and well-developed, featuring a variety of shops, restaurants, and cultural experiences, all designed to cater to cruise passengers. From here, visitors can easily access nearby attractions like the Falmouth Heritage Walk, local beaches, and the many tour operators offering excursions.

Transportation options in Falmouth are plentiful. Taxis and private drivers are available for hire directly from the port or from designated taxi stands. For those who prefer to explore the area at their own pace, renting a car is a good option, though it's important to note that driving is on the left side of the road in Jamaica. For those staying at resorts, many offer shuttle services to and from the cruise port. If you're heading to more distant attractions like the Luminous Lagoon or

Martha Brae River, guided tours are available, which provide round-trip transportation and knowledgeable guides who share insights into the island's culture and history.

When planning your visit to Falmouth, it's important to keep the operating hours of major attractions in mind. Many attractions are open year-round, though it's worth noting that some, like the Luminous Lagoon tours, are best experienced at night. Seasonal considerations are important as well—during the peak tourist season (December through April), the town and its attractions can be quite crowded, so early morning visits are recommended to avoid the heaviest crowds. During the off-season (May through November), the weather can be more humid, with a higher chance of rain, but it also means fewer visitors and a more relaxed atmosphere.

For travelers looking for local insights and hidden gems in Falmouth, consider visiting the nearby Good Hope Estate. Located just a short drive from the town, Good Hope offers a glimpse into the life of a sugar plantation, with well-preserved colonial architecture, nature trails, and a river for tubing and rafting. It's an excellent option for those seeking a peaceful retreat with a historical twist. Another lesser-known gem is the Falmouth Market, where local artisans and vendors sell handmade crafts, fresh produce, and vibrant Jamaican spices.

Safety in Falmouth is generally good, but like any tourist destination, it's essential to take basic precautions. Stick to well-populated areas, particularly after dark, and always use registered taxis for transportation. It's also advisable to avoid engaging with aggressive street vendors and to watch your belongings in crowded areas.

Accessibility features in Falmouth are improving, with some attractions offering wheelchair access. However, it's important to check in advance, especially if you plan to visit sites like the Martha Brae River or Luminous Lagoon, which may not have full accessibility.

Falmouth, Jamaica, offers cruise passengers a rich, vibrant experience that combines the island's deep historical roots with its modern-day hospitality and natural beauty. Whether you're wandering through the historic streets of the town, enjoying the glow of the Luminous Lagoon, or sampling delicious local dishes, Falmouth is a port that provides diverse experiences for every traveler. To truly appreciate all that Falmouth has to offer, venture beyond the typical tourist spots and discover the hidden gems that reflect the authentic heart and soul of Jamaica.

Roatán, Honduras

Roatán, Honduras, is a tropical paradise located in the Caribbean Sea, just off the northern coast of Honduras. It is the largest of the Bay Islands, part of a small archipelago known for its stunning natural beauty, vibrant culture, and warm, friendly locals. Roatán is a well-known cruise stop, offering visitors a unique blend of lush landscapes, crystal-clear waters, rich marine life, and a laid-back Caribbean atmosphere. It has become a sought-after destination for those seeking both relaxation and adventure.

Roatán's cultural diversity is another key feature of the island, with influences from the indigenous Garífuna people, Afro-Caribbean descendants, and Spanish colonizers. Over time, the island's identity has been shaped by these diverse groups, creating a dynamic blend of traditions, music, and cuisine that makes Roatán's culture unique. It's a place where the colorful Caribbean spirit meets the traditions of its varied peoples, resulting in an island that is both inviting and rich in heritage.

Roatán's charm lies not just in its natural beauty, but in the variety of experiences it offers to travelers. The island is famous for its world-class diving, with some of the most diverse coral reefs in the world. The Mesoamerican Reef provides a stunning underwater landscape, teeming with vibrant coral, tropical fish, and larger marine life such as turtles and rays. Popular dive sites such as the Mary's Place dive site and the Blue Channel offer exhilarating dives for experienced divers, while the shallow reefs are perfect for beginners.

For those preferring land-based activities, Roatán offers plenty of options. West Bay Beach is a standout, offering soft white sand, turquoise waters, and a lively atmosphere. It's one of the most popular beaches on the island, with many beachside resorts and restaurants. For a more peaceful experience, head to the quieter East End of the island, where the scenery is just as breathtaking, but the crowds are thinner. Hiking trails, such as those leading to the top of the island's hills, provide stunning panoramic views of the Caribbean and the surrounding islands.

Another must-see attraction on the island is the Carambola Gardens, which offers visitors the opportunity to walk through lush tropical landscapes while learning about the island's unique flora and fauna. The Roatán Institute for Marine Sciences (RIMS) is also a popular stop, where visitors can learn more about the island's marine life and conservation efforts.

For those interested in cultural activities, a visit to the Garífuna village in the West End is a chance to experience the island's indigenous roots. The Garífuna people are known for their music, dance, and storytelling, and you can often hear the sound of drums in the air as they perform traditional dances. Roatán is also home to the Ixchel Art Gallery, where visitors can experience local art, jewelry, and crafts, offering a unique way to support local artisans.

In terms of local cuisine, Roatán is a treat for food lovers. Traditional Honduran dishes such as "baleadas" (flour tortillas filled with beans, cheese, and cream) and "tamalitos" (steamed cornmeal dough with fillings) are popular across the island. Seafood is also a staple, with fresh fish, shrimp, and lobster available at most local restaurants. "Sopa de caracol" (conch soup) is another local specialty, offering a rich, flavorful taste of the island. For an authentic experience, try dining at a local restaurant like the "The Lighthouse Restaurant," known for its fresh seafood and picturesque views, or head to "Creole's Rotisserie Chicken" for a casual meal with delicious Caribbean flavors.

Cruise ships dock at the Coxen Hole Port, which is located on the island's southern side. This port is relatively close to the island's main attractions, including the town of West End and West Bay Beach. The port area features a small shopping complex with artisan shops, bars, and restaurants catering to cruise passengers. From here, visitors can easily access transportation to the island's various attractions.

Transportation options on Roatán are abundant. Taxis are widely available at the port and throughout the island, though it's a good idea to negotiate prices before starting a journey. Private transportation services and shuttle buses are also available, particularly for those going on tours. Renting a car is another option, though be prepared for the island's steep hills and narrow roads. Many hotels and resorts also offer shuttle services for their guests. Roatán's public transportation system is limited, so taxis and private vehicles remain the most reliable mode of travel for visitors.

When planning a visit to Roatán, it's important to keep seasonal considerations in mind. The best time to visit is between December and April, which is the dry season on the island. During these months, the weather is pleasant, and you can enjoy outdoor activities like hiking, snorkeling, and diving. The off-season from May to November is the wet season, though rainfall is often brief and does not typically disrupt activities. However, visitors during this time should be prepared for more humidity and the possibility of hurricanes, which can affect travel plans.

For those visiting Roatán, it's worth noting a few safety tips. While the island is generally safe for tourists, it's always best to stick to well-populated areas, especially at night. Avoid displaying expensive items like jewelry or cameras in more secluded spots. As with any tropical destination, be cautious of strong currents when swimming or snorkeling, especially in areas like West Bay Beach.

For visitors with disabilities, Roatán's accessibility features are slowly improving, with some hotels and attractions offering wheelchair access. However, the island's terrain can be hilly and uneven, so travelers with mobility issues may need to plan their trips carefully.

Roatán has several hidden gems that many visitors miss. For example, the Paya Bay Beach, located on the island's eastern side, is far less crowded than West Bay and offers pristine sand and clear waters. Another hidden gem is the "Little French Key" private island, a short boat ride away from the main island. It's a great spot for those seeking a more intimate beach experience with plenty of activities, including kayaking, paddleboarding, and snorkeling.

Roatán, Honduras, offers a rich blend of natural beauty, adventure, culture, and history, making it a perfect destination for cruise passengers. Whether you're exploring the vibrant underwater world, lounging on quiet beaches, enjoying the local cuisine, or immersing yourself in the island's cultural heritage, Roatán provides a wealth of experiences that showcase the heart and soul of the Bay Islands. By venturing beyond the well-trodden tourist paths, travelers can uncover the true essence of Roatán and experience a destination that is as diverse as it is captivating.

CHAPTER 5.
SOUTHERN CARIBBEAN PORTS

Bridgetown, Barbados

Bridgetown, the vibrant capital of Barbados, is an unmissable destination for cruise passengers exploring the Caribbean. Located on the southwestern coast of the island, Bridgetown is the island's hub for commerce, culture, and history. With its stunning coastal views, tropical climate, and rich blend of Caribbean, African, and European influences, Bridgetown offers visitors a unique insight into the island's culture and heritage. The city is situated along the sheltered Carlisle Bay, which makes it a natural port of call for cruise ships, and it also has easy access to some of the island's most beautiful beaches, gardens, and historical landmarks.

One of the most striking features of Bridgetown is its multicultural atmosphere. Its history as a colonial port, combined with the traditions of African, Caribbean, and European heritage, creates a blend of cultures reflected in the city's architecture, festivals, cuisine, and daily life. Bridgetown's significance lies not only in its role as the capital but also as a symbol of Barbados' deep-rooted identity as a nation that has evolved from indigenous settlements through European colonization to its current vibrant, independent state.

Key attractions in Bridgetown include a range of historical, cultural, and natural sites. The Garrison Historic Area is one of the most significant parts of the city, with its beautiful Georgian architecture and landmarks like the Barbados Museum, the old Military Prison, and the historic Clock Tower. Another highlight is Bridgetown and its surroundings, including the Careenage, which is an old harbor area now lined with colorful buildings, restaurants, and shops. The area has a relaxed, cosmopolitan vibe, and it's a great place to enjoy the atmosphere while watching boats sail by. The nearby Parliament Buildings, another important historical landmark, are home to the seat of Barbados' government and offer free tours to visitors keen to learn more about the island's political history.

For those looking to experience nature, there are plenty of options. The island's botanical gardens, such as the Andromeda Botanic Gardens, showcase the island's lush flora and provide a peaceful retreat from the hustle and bustle of the city. Carlisle Bay is another must-visit location for anyone looking to enjoy the island's famous beaches. The bay is not only home to a stunning beach but also offers fantastic snorkeling and diving opportunities with its abundant marine life and shipwrecks. Visitors can take a catamaran cruise around the bay or rent a jet ski for some action-packed fun.

In terms of local cuisine, Bridgetown has an array of dining options that will appeal to all tastes. Barbadian cuisine, often referred to as Bajan cuisine, is a flavorful fusion of African, British, and Caribbean influences. Some of the island's signature dishes include flying fish (often served fried or steamed), cou cou (cornmeal and okra), and pepperpot (a hearty stew made with meat and vegetables). Oistins Fish Fry, located in the southern part of the island near Bridgetown, is a must-see for food lovers. This lively outdoor market and restaurant complex offers fresh seafood cooked to order, with a lively atmosphere enhanced by local music and dancing. For a more refined dining experience, check out The Cliff, one of the island's most renowned restaurants, offering gourmet food and a stunning view of the ocean.

Cruise ships dock at the Bridgetown Port, located close to the heart of the city. The port is easily accessible from the main attractions, and visitors will find it simple to explore the area on foot or by using local transport options. One of the most popular forms of transportation around Bridgetown is the public "ZRs" (small minibuses) and buses, which are cheap and frequent. Taxis are also readily available, though it's advisable to agree on a price before embarking. For those preferring a more comfortable experience, hotel shuttles and organized tours are available, particularly for those seeking to explore the more remote areas of the island.

As with many tropical destinations, the best time to visit Bridgetown is during the dry season, which runs from December to April. This period sees the most pleasant weather, with sunny days and lower humidity. However, it's also the busiest time of year, especially during Christmas and spring break, so expect larger crowds at popular attractions. The off-season, from May to November, offers fewer tourists, but there is a higher chance of rain and potential hurricanes, so visitors should keep an eye on the weather forecast during this time.

Safety in Bridgetown is generally not a major concern, though like any busy tourist destination, it's wise to stay alert. Avoid isolated areas after dark, and be cautious when handling money and valuables in crowded spots. It's always a good idea to use reputable taxi services or arrange transportation through your hotel. For those with disabilities, Bridgetown offers some accessibility options, though it's worth noting that many of the city's attractions, such as historic sites, may not have full wheelchair access. However, newer developments and certain tour operators have made strides in providing accessible facilities.

Bridgetown is not only known for its major attractions but also for its hidden gems that locals cherish. One such place is the St. Nicholas Abbey, an old plantation house located a little outside the city. This site offers insight into the island's sugar cane history and allows visitors to experience the authentic rum-making process at one of the island's oldest distilleries. Another off-the-beaten-path recommendation is the Graeme Hall Nature Sanctuary, a peaceful sanctuary for birdwatchers and nature lovers. It's a tranquil spot that provides a rare glimpse into the island's wildlife and natural beauty, far from the hustle of the city center.

Bridgetown, Barbados, is a delightful port of call that blends Caribbean charm with rich history, stunning landscapes, and a vibrant cultural scene. Whether you're strolling through its historic streets, tasting its delicious food, or exploring its natural beauty, Bridgetown offers something for every type of traveler. For cruise passengers, it's an ideal destination to dive into the local culture, savor delicious food, and enjoy the laid-back yet lively spirit of the island. So, be sure to explore beyond the typical tourist paths to fully appreciate the multifaceted charm of this Caribbean gem.

Oranjestad, Aruba

Oranjestad, the capital city of Aruba, is a vibrant and culturally rich destination that welcomes cruise passengers with its unique blend of Caribbean charm, Dutch colonial history, and modern luxury. Located on the southwestern coast of the island, Oranjestad is the heart of Aruba's economy, culture, and tourism. Its colorful buildings, waterfront views, and lively atmosphere make it a memorable stop for anyone cruising the Caribbean.

The city is geographically significant, situated along a sheltered harbor, making it a natural port for ships to dock.

This proximity to both the sea and Aruba's inland natural beauty makes Oranjestad an ideal gateway for visitors to experience the island's diverse offerings. The city has a distinct mix of European and Caribbean influences, with Dutch colonial architecture blending seamlessly with the island's more vibrant Caribbean spirit.

Oranjestad is a multicultural hub, reflecting the diverse heritage of the island's population, which includes Afro-Caribbean, Dutch, and Latin American influences. This cultural diversity is evident in the city's festivals, food, and day-to-day life. The city's blend of old-world European charm and lively Caribbean energy makes it a dynamic and inviting destination.

Key attractions and activities in Oranjestad are varied, offering something for everyone. For history enthusiasts, a visit to Fort Zoutman is a must. Another key historical site is the National Archaeological Museum, which showcases artifacts from Aruba's indigenous Arawak culture, as well as displays on the island's Dutch colonial history. For those looking to explore the natural beauty of the island, the nearby Arikok National Park offers hiking trails, stunning views, and an opportunity to see Aruba's unique flora and fauna. The park is also home to cave paintings that date back thousands of years, adding a fascinating cultural layer to any visit.

For a taste of island life, head to the colorful shopping district of Oranjestad. The city's streets are lined with boutiques, duty-free shops, and jewelry stores, offering visitors a chance to pick up local crafts, clothing, and souvenirs. While shopping, you can take in the city's signature pastel-colored buildings, which add to the laid-back, welcoming vibe of the area. In addition, the waterfront area is perfect for taking a relaxing stroll, with plenty of cafes and bars offering views of the harbor.

When it comes to dining, Oranjestad offers a variety of options that reflect the island's cultural diversity. The local cuisine is a delicious fusion of Caribbean, Dutch, and Latin flavors. A must-try dish is "keshi yena," a flavorful casserole made with chicken, beef, or fish and stuffed into a cheese shell. Another popular dish is "pastechi," a savory pastry filled with cheese, beef, or chicken. For those looking to sample the island's seafood, fresh fish is a staple at many of the waterfront restaurants.

One of the best spots to sample local flavors is the Old Dutch Windmill Restaurant, which offers both Caribbean and Dutch-inspired dishes. For a more casual experience, try the Seaport Marketplace, where vendors offer fresh seafood and other local dishes in a lively, open-air setting. For dessert, be sure to try a piece of Aruban coconut cake or "Tanki Lele," a local rum-based drink.

When arriving in Oranjestad, most cruise ships dock at the main port, which is located just a short walk from the city center. The proximity of the port to the heart of the city makes it easy for visitors to explore the sights on foot. Alternatively, taxis and shuttles are readily available to take passengers to nearby attractions, beaches, and resorts. Public transportation on the island is relatively straightforward, with buses running to popular destinations across the island. For those looking for a more scenic journey, many visitors choose to rent a bike or scooter to explore the island at their own pace.

Operating hours for major attractions in Oranjestad vary, but most sites are open from 9:00 AM to 5:00 PM. However, many shops and restaurants stay open later, particularly in the evenings when the city comes alive with music and events. During the high season, which runs from December to April, Oranjestad sees a surge in visitors, making it a good time to enjoy the city's festivals, markets, and local celebrations. The off-season, from May to November, offers fewer crowds, but there is a higher chance of rain and occasional hurricanes, so travelers should plan accordingly.

For visitors, the best times to visit Oranjestad are typically in the early morning or late afternoon, when the temperatures are cooler, and the streets are less crowded. To avoid the heat of midday, plan to take part in activities like shopping or visiting museums early in the day, while reserving outdoor adventures like hiking or visiting the beach for later in the afternoon.

In terms of safety, Oranjestad is generally very safe for tourists, though, as with any popular tourist destination, it's important to stay alert. Petty theft, such as pickpocketing, can occasionally occur in busy areas, so it's advisable to keep valuables secure. Stick to well-lit areas in the evening, and avoid venturing too far from the main streets at night. Additionally, Aruba's excellent public health and safety systems ensure that visitors can rely on local services if needed.

For travelers with disabilities, Oranjestad is a relatively accessible city. Many of the main attractions, such as the National Archaeological Museum, are wheelchair accessible, and most public transportation options can accommodate those with mobility challenges. However, some of the island's more natural areas, like Arikok National Park, may have limited accessibility due to uneven terrain.

Hidden gems in Oranjestad that many visitors might miss include the Wilhelmina Park, a peaceful green space filled with sculptures and local plants. It's a great place to relax and enjoy the island's natural beauty. Another lesser-known spot is Renaissance Island, a private resort island that offers an exclusive, serene beach experience just a short boat ride from the city center.

Oranjestad, Aruba, is a vibrant, welcoming city that offers a perfect blend of history, culture, natural beauty, and modern amenities. Whether you're exploring its colonial landmarks, enjoying its lively shopping scene, or indulging in its unique cuisine, the city has something for everyone. For cruise passengers, Oranjestad is an enriching stop that provides a deep dive into the heart of Aruba, offering plenty of opportunities to explore its rich cultural fabric, historical significance, and breathtaking landscapes.

Willemstad, Curaçao

Willemstad, the capital of Curaçao, is a port city that effortlessly blends history, culture, and natural beauty, making it a captivating stop for cruise passengers. Situated on the southern coast of the island in the Caribbean Sea, Willemstad is renowned for its vibrant and colorful Dutch colonial architecture, UNESCO World Heritage status, and its role as a major historical and cultural hub in the region.

Willemstad's cultural diversity is one of its most striking features. The city reflects the island's rich history, influenced by indigenous peoples, African slaves, Dutch colonizers, and waves of European and Asian migrants. This cultural melting pot is visible in the city's festivals, music, language, and cuisine. Visitors will hear the local Papiamento language, a unique Creole that blends Portuguese, Spanish, Dutch, and African influences, and experience the warmth and hospitality of its people.

Willemstad's historical significance is preserved in various landmarks throughout the city. A visit to the famous floating bridge, known as the Queen Emma Bridge, is an iconic experience. The bridge, which opens to allow ships to pass through the harbor, is a testament to the city's unique engineering and maritime history. The Kura Hulanda Museum, located in the heart of the city, offers a profound exploration of the African slave trade and the island's history of slavery and emancipation. The museum is housed in a restored 18th-century complex and provides a deep dive into the painful history that shaped much of the island's culture.

Key attractions in Willemstad are numerous and cater to a variety of interests. The Punda district is the historic heart of the city, featuring charming streets lined with shops, cafes, and restaurants. Here, visitors can explore attractions like the Mikvé Israel-Emanuel Synagogue, the oldest synagogue in continuous use in the Americas, and the Willemstad Harbor, which offers scenic views of the city's waterfront. For those interested in nature, a trip to the nearby Christoffel National Park is a must. The park is home to diverse wildlife, hiking trails, and the island's highest peak, Christoffel Mountain, which offers panoramic views of the surrounding landscape.

Curaçao's beaches are also a big draw for visitors, and Willemstad is the perfect launching point for exploring the island's pristine coastline. Popular beaches such as Playa Knip and Cas Abao Beach are just a short drive away and offer crystal-clear waters ideal for swimming, snorkeling, and diving. The surrounding waters also boast impressive coral reefs, making the area a popular spot for water sports and marine life enthusiasts.

For those interested in local cuisine, Willemstad is a gastronomic delight. The city's restaurants offer a blend of Caribbean, Dutch, and Latin American flavors. A local specialty to try is "stoba," a flavorful stew made with beef, goat, or chicken, and served with rice and vegetables. The island's seafood is also exceptional, with fresh fish, conch, and shrimp featured in many dishes. For a more casual dining experience, head to the floating market, where vendors sell fresh produce, seafood, and local products straight from Venezuela.

A great dining option for visitors is Plasa Bieu, a food court where local vendors serve up traditional dishes such as "funchi" (cornmeal porridge) and "keshi yena," a stuffed cheese dish. For a more upscale experience, visit the restaurant at the Avila Beach Hotel, where guests can enjoy a fusion of Caribbean and international cuisine with an ocean view. If you're looking for a refreshing drink, the local cocktail, the "Blue Curaçao," is a must-try. This vibrant blue liqueur is made from the island's native laraha fruit and is often enjoyed in tropical cocktails.

When visiting Willemstad, most cruise ships dock at the main harbor, which is conveniently located within walking distance of the Punda district. This makes it easy for passengers to step off the ship and dive straight into exploring the city's vibrant streets, historic landmarks, and shopping areas. There are also shuttle services and taxis available at the dock, which can take visitors to further-reaching attractions like beaches or the Christoffel National Park.

Getting around Willemstad is relatively easy. The city's compact size makes it ideal for walking, and most of the key attractions are close together. Taxis are available for trips outside the city center, and buses run regularly to various parts of the island. Many visitors also opt to rent a car for more flexibility in exploring the island's beaches and nature reserves. For those looking for a more unique mode of transport, renting a scooter or bicycle is a fun way to explore the city at your own pace.

The operating hours of attractions in Willemstad generally run from 9:00 AM to 5:00 PM, though some shops and restaurants may stay open later, especially in the evenings when the city comes alive with music, dining, and entertainment. The peak tourist season in Willemstad runs from December to April, during which the weather is more comfortable and the city hosts numerous festivals and cultural events. The off-season, from May to November, sees fewer crowds, but travelers should be mindful of the potential for rain and hurricanes during this period.

For those visiting Willemstad, the best times to explore the city are early in the morning or late afternoon, when temperatures are cooler, and crowds are thinner. It's advisable to visit popular attractions such as the floating market or the Willemstad Harbor early to avoid large crowds. The evenings are also a great time to explore the city, as Willemstad takes on a magical atmosphere with its illuminated buildings and bustling outdoor cafes.

Willemstad is considered a safe destination for travelers. However, as in any major tourist hub, it's important to be vigilant against petty theft. Avoid carrying large sums of cash or valuables in busy areas, and be mindful of your surroundings. For visitors concerned about accessibility, Willemstad is a relatively accessible city, with many attractions being wheelchair-friendly. However, some of the more natural areas and beaches may have limited access due to uneven terrain.

Willemstad also boasts a few hidden gems that offer a deeper dive into the island's culture and natural beauty. One such gem is the Landhuis Chobolobo, the historic distillery where Blue Curaçao liqueur is made. Visitors can tour the distillery and sample the local product. Another hidden gem is the serene Jan Thiel Beach, which offers a quieter alternative to some of the more crowded beaches around Willemstad. The area is perfect for a peaceful day of sunbathing and swimming.

Willemstad is a port that offers a rich tapestry of experiences for cruise passengers, from its colorful streets and rich cultural history to its pristine beaches and delicious cuisine. Whether you're walking through its UNESCO World Heritage-listed streets, learning about its colonial past, or enjoying the island's unique food and drinks, Willemstad offers something for every type of traveler. By venturing beyond the popular tourist spots and discovering the island's hidden gems, you can truly appreciate the diverse cultures and histories that make this city such a captivating destination.

St. George's, Grenada

St. George's, Grenada, is a stunning port city located on the west coast of the island, known for its picturesque harbor, colorful colonial architecture, and lush hillsides that embrace the Caribbean Sea. Grenada, often referred to as the "Spice Isle," is celebrated for its spice plantations, particularly nutmeg, and St. George's is the island's vibrant heart. Its geographical significance as a natural harbor has made it a key maritime hub throughout history, while its laid-back atmosphere and stunning scenery make it a unique stop for cruise passengers.

The city is not only a tropical paradise but also a cultural crossroads, blending Afro-Caribbean heritage with French, British, and indigenous influences. This mix of cultures has created a warm, welcoming environment where visitors can immerse themselves in local traditions, food, and music. St. George's is also known for its thriving arts scene, bustling markets, and historical landmarks, all of which offer a glimpse into the island's rich heritage.

St. George's offers a variety of attractions and activities that cater to all types of visitors. One of the most notable landmarks is the Carenage, the harbor of St. George's, which is lined with colorful Georgian buildings. The area is perfect for leisurely strolls, boat rides, and taking in views of the bustling port. The area around the Carenage also features several historic sites, including the Grenada National Museum, located in the old French colonial building. The museum showcases Grenada's history, from its indigenous Carib and Arawak peoples to the island's colonial past and its fight for independence.

For panoramic views of the city and its surroundings, visitors should head to Fort George, perched on a hilltop overlooking the harbor. This 18th-century fort, which once protected the island from naval threats, is now a historical site that provides visitors with a taste of Grenada's military history, along with breathtaking vistas of the town below. Another must-see is Fort Frederick, another historic fortification that offers spectacular views of the harbor and the Caribbean Sea. It's a quieter spot compared to Fort George, but equally stunning in terms of scenery and historical interest.

Nature lovers will find plenty to explore in the vicinity of St. George's, including the beautiful Annandale Falls, a series of waterfalls nestled in the lush rainforest. Visitors can take guided hikes through the surrounding nature trails, where they will encounter local flora and fauna, including tropical birds, exotic plants, and colorful butterflies. Another hidden gem is the Grand Anse Beach, located just a short drive from the city center. This iconic beach is perfect for relaxation, swimming, and water sports, with crystal-clear waters and soft sand.

The spice plantations surrounding St. George's offer unique, guided tours where visitors can see how nutmeg, cloves, cinnamon, and other spices are grown, harvested, and processed. These tours provide insight into the island's rich agricultural history and are a fantastic way to experience Grenada's natural beauty.

Grenada's cuisine is a delightful reflection of its diverse cultural influences, with flavors that range from spicy and savory to sweet and fragrant. Local dishes to try include "oil down," a hearty one-pot dish made with salted meat, dumplings, breadfruit, and vegetables, cooked in coconut milk. Another must-try is "callaloo," a green soup made with leafy vegetables and coconut milk, often served with crab or fish. For a taste of Grenada's spice culture, try a dish with "scotch bonnet peppers," which give the food a distinct heat and flavor.

For a more casual, yet authentic, dining experience, head to the local market in St. George's, where you can sample fresh fruit, seafood, and spices directly from the vendors. The bustling atmosphere of the market is a fantastic way to immerse yourself in the local culture. For sit-down meals, try restaurants such as The Aquarium Restaurant, located by the beach, which offers Caribbean seafood and tropical cocktails, or the popular BB's Crabback, which serves fresh local seafood with a scenic view of the harbor.

When visiting St. George's, most cruise ships dock at the Port Louis Marina, located within walking distance of the town center. The marina is the perfect spot to disembark and start exploring the charming streets of St. George's, with its historic buildings, lively shops, and local cafes. Taxis, minibuses, and private car services are readily available for visitors wishing to explore farther, such as beaches or the spice plantations. The city is also small enough that you can easily navigate on foot, with most attractions within a short walking distance from the dock.

Operating hours for major attractions in St. George's typically run from 9:00 AM to 5:00 PM, but it's best to check specific sites for any variations, especially during holidays or festivals. The best time to visit is between December and April when the weather is dry and sunny, although this is also the peak tourist season. If you prefer fewer crowds, visiting during the off-season from May to November can provide a more laid-back experience, although visitors should be aware of the occasional rain showers and the potential for hurricanes.

To make the most of your time in St. George's, try to visit popular attractions like Fort George and the Carenage early in the morning to avoid crowds. Mid-afternoon is a great time for a beach trip, as the sun is at its peak. Evening strolls along the waterfront or in the town center are equally enjoyable, with local vendors and musicians adding to the lively atmosphere.

St. George's is a safe and welcoming destination for travelers, though it's always wise to remain aware of your surroundings in busy tourist areas. Petty theft can occasionally occur in crowded spots, so it's recommended not to carry too much cash or valuables while sightseeing. For those with mobility challenges, most of the city's main attractions, such as the museum and Carenage, are wheelchair accessible, though the steep streets and narrow sidewalks may present some challenges.

For those looking to experience St. George's in a more intimate way, consider visiting some of the hidden gems recommended by locals. For example, the Belmont Estate offers a tour of a traditional cocoa plantation where you can learn about Grenada's chocolate-making process and even sample freshly made chocolate. Another lesser-known gem is the True Blue Bay, a quiet and peaceful spot away from the crowds, ideal for kayaking or enjoying a sunset.

St. George's, Grenada, is a rich tapestry of history, culture, and natural beauty, offering a variety of experiences for cruise passengers. Whether you're exploring the city's historic forts, strolling through its colorful streets, or relaxing on its pristine beaches, St. George's is a destination that leaves a lasting impression. By venturing beyond the typical tourist paths and embracing the local culture, visitors can uncover the true spirit of Grenada.

CHAPTER 6.
PRIVATE ISLANDS AND EXCLUSIVE STOPS

CocoCay, Bahamas (Royal Caribbean)

CocoCay, located in the Bahamas, is a private island owned and operated by Royal Caribbean International. This tropical paradise is designed specifically to cater to the needs of cruise passengers, offering a laid-back, exclusive experience. CocoCay lies just off the coast of Great Abaco Island in the northern part of the Bahamas, roughly 55 miles from Nassau, the capital of the Bahamas. The island is only accessible to passengers on Royal Caribbean ships, making it an exclusive and serene destination for those looking for relaxation and adventure. With its crystal-clear waters, white sand beaches, and a plethora of activities, CocoCay is a sought-after stop on many Caribbean cruise itineraries.

CocoCay is not only a stunning tropical destination but also a place that reflects the beauty and cultural diversity of the Bahamas. The island's primary purpose is to serve as a luxurious escape for cruise guests, with many features designed to blend seamlessly with its natural surroundings. The culture of CocoCay is rooted in the Bahamian way of life, which is characterized by friendliness, music, and hospitality. While the island is privately operated by Royal Caribbean, the cultural heritage of the Bahamas remains an important aspect, with local crafts, food, and entertainment often reflecting the traditions of the Bahamian people.

Historically, CocoCay was originally known as Little Stirrup Cay and had been used by various groups throughout its history, including indigenous peoples, pirates, and early European settlers. However, it was Royal Caribbean's development of the island into a private resort destination in the 1990s that transformed it into the idyllic getaway it is today. Over the years, the island has undergone several upgrades and enhancements, including the addition of upscale amenities, waterparks, and a variety of dining and recreational options designed to provide guests with an all-inclusive experience.

For those visiting CocoCay, there are a number of must-see attractions and activities that cater to all types of travelers, whether you're seeking relaxation, adventure, or cultural experiences. One of the main highlights is Perfect Day at CocoCay, a major development that has transformed the island into an all-encompassing resort. It features the largest freshwater pool in the Caribbean, which is a great spot to cool off and swim while enjoying a panoramic view of the island. The pool area also includes a swim-up bar for those looking to enjoy a tropical drink while lounging in the water.

For thrill-seekers, The Thrill Waterpark is an exhilarating experience with numerous water slides, a wave pool, and even a tower that offers an adrenaline-pumping zip line ride. Families will love the Splashaway Bay water play area, designed specifically for children, where they can enjoy fountains, slides, and water jets. The island also offers Coco Beach Club, an exclusive area for adults who want a more peaceful, luxurious beach experience with private cabanas, an infinity pool, and upscale dining options.

If you're interested in exploring the island's natural beauty, CocoCay's beaches are some of the best in the Bahamas. The pristine white sand is perfect for lounging, and the calm turquoise waters are ideal for swimming, snorkeling, and even kayaking. Snorkeling excursions are available where you can explore the colorful underwater world just off the shore, encountering tropical fish and vibrant coral reefs. For those looking to venture further out, stingray and dolphin encounters are also offered as unique experiences for nature lovers.

The local cuisine at CocoCay showcases the best of Bahamian flavors, with many of the food options served in relaxed, beachside settings. The Chill Grill is the main dining venue on the island, offering a variety of buffet-style meals that include grilled meats, local seafood, and tropical fruits. It's the perfect spot to refuel after a day of sun and sea. For a more exclusive dining experience, guests can head to the Coco Beach Club, where they can enjoy gourmet dishes with an ocean view. The menu here often features fresh seafood, Caribbean-inspired dishes, and signature cocktails.

CocoCay's offerings are designed for cruise passengers, so docking is straightforward. Royal Caribbean's ships dock directly at the island, and there's no need for tendering or using other boats to reach the island. Cruise ships dock at CocoCay's pier, which is conveniently located near many of the island's attractions. Once docked, passengers are free to explore the island and enjoy the various activities available.

Getting around the island is easy, as most of the main attractions are within walking distance of the docking area. However, there are also trams available to transport passengers to the farthest reaches of the island, especially if you are heading to the more secluded beaches or the waterpark. You won't need a rental car or taxi on CocoCay, as everything is accessible by foot or the provided transportation options.

Operating hours for most attractions on CocoCay align with the cruise ship schedules, so visitors can enjoy the island from the time the ship docks until it departs. Major attractions like the waterpark, beach club, and dining facilities are typically open during the day, often from around 9 AM to 5 PM. However, specific operating hours may vary depending on the time of year, so it's advisable to check with the cruise line for any updates.

For those planning to visit CocoCay, it's best to arrive early in the day to avoid the crowds, especially if you're interested in enjoying the popular activities like the waterpark or beach club, which can become crowded during peak times. Mid-morning or early afternoon is also a good time to visit the more relaxing areas, such as the beaches or the pool areas, for a quieter experience. To avoid the summer heat, consider visiting during the cooler months (November to April), but keep in mind that this is also peak cruise season.

As with any destination, there are some safety considerations to keep in mind while visiting CocoCay. The island is generally very safe, but it's important to stay vigilant when in crowded areas or when purchasing items from local vendors. Be aware of prices for activities or souvenirs, as they can sometimes be higher on the island than in Nassau or other parts of the Bahamas. Always check prices and confirm the total cost before making a purchase or booking an excursion. While the island is relatively easy to navigate, the tropical environment means sunburns and dehydration can happen quickly. It's important to stay hydrated and apply sunscreen throughout the day.

Accessibility features are also considered on CocoCay, with many attractions, including the beaches and waterpark, being accessible to guests with mobility challenges. The island's transportation system includes trams, and the walking paths are generally well-maintained, making it easier for those with limited mobility to get around.

For hidden gems, consider exploring Gloat Bay, a more secluded area on the island that offers a tranquil atmosphere away from the crowds. You can also try visiting the CocoCay Observation Tower for panoramic views of the island and surrounding sea, an experience that many visitors miss but is well worth the climb.

In conclusion, CocoCay, Bahamas (Royal Caribbean) offers an exciting and relaxing experience for cruise passengers. Whether you're seeking adventure in the waterpark, relaxing on the beach, or immersing yourself in Bahamian cuisine and culture, CocoCay provides something for everyone. The island's unique combination of natural beauty, exclusive amenities, and vibrant Bahamian spirit ensures that every visit is memorable. For travelers looking to unwind and enjoy a private island experience, CocoCay is an exceptional destination.

Half Moon Cay, Bahamas (Holland America Line)

Half Moon Cay, located in the Bahamas, is a private island exclusively used by Holland America Line. This serene island lies approximately 100 miles southeast of Nassau and is part of the Out Islands of the Bahamas, known for their untouched natural beauty and tranquil atmosphere. Unlike the more developed areas of the Bahamas, Half Moon Cay offers a peaceful retreat with soft white sand beaches, crystal-clear turquoise waters, and a laid-back vibe, making it a perfect stop for cruise passengers seeking a tropical getaway. Its unique blend of relaxation and adventure, combined with its exclusive access to Holland America Line passengers, sets it apart from other Caribbean destinations.

Half Moon Cay is often referred to as a "perfect" private island escape because of its pristine environment and lack of overcrowding. While the island is primarily visited by Holland America ships, it still exudes the warm and welcoming culture of the Bahamas. Bahamian traditions and influences can be seen throughout the island, from the food and music to the island's design and decor. The local community does not reside on Half Moon Cay, but the island is owned and operated by Holland America Line, with a dedicated staff from the Bahamas providing services, making it an authentic and culturally-rich experience for visitors.

Historically, Half Moon Cay was originally known as Little San Salvador Island. The island has a rich history, with roots dating back to the indigenous Lucayan people, who inhabited the Bahamas long before European explorers arrived. The island later became a strategic stopover for European ships during the Age of Exploration.

For visitors, Half Moon Cay offers an array of must-see attractions and activities that cater to both relaxation and adventure. The Beaches are the primary draw, with the island's Half Moon Beach being particularly famous for its crescent-shaped, powdery white sands and crystal-clear waters. It's an idyllic location for sunbathing, swimming, or simply enjoying the stunning views of the ocean.

Beyond the beach, visitors can explore a number of exciting activities. Snorkeling is a popular option, with several locations on the island offering access to vibrant coral reefs and colorful marine life. You can rent equipment or take part in guided snorkeling excursions to explore the underwater world, where you might encounter tropical fish, rays, and even sea turtles. Kayaking and paddleboarding are also available, providing an excellent way to explore the serene waters around the island. For those who prefer more active pursuits, horseback riding along the beach offers a unique experience, as riders can enjoy the beauty of the island from a different perspective.

For thrill-seekers, the island also offers aerial adventures. The Aqua Park is another favorite, featuring inflatables and obstacles set up in the water for an active and fun experience. Visitors can also embark on eco-tours, where they can explore the natural landscape of the island, including its native flora and fauna.

In addition to these outdoor adventures, Half Moon Cay has a Cultural Village where you can learn about Bahamian culture. There are local craft shops where visitors can purchase handmade goods such as jewelry, clothing, and souvenirs crafted by Bahamian artisans. Many guests also take advantage of the Bahamas-style barbecue, an authentic culinary experience served beachfront. It's a wonderful opportunity to enjoy local seafood, jerk chicken, and Bahamian-style conch fritters.

When it comes to dining, Half Moon Cay offers several options, but the buffet-style BBQ on the beach is a must-try. The island's main dining area, the Lido Restaurant, serves a wide variety of delicious Bahamian and international dishes, including fresh fish, grilled meats, and tropical fruits. The food is fresh, flavorful, and reflective of Bahamian culture. If you're looking for a more relaxed and scenic experience, the Private Cabanas provide an intimate dining option with personalized service, giving you the chance to enjoy a meal while overlooking the beach.

Half Moon Cay is designed specifically to cater to cruise passengers, and its dock is right on the island, making access easy and direct from the cruise ship. The island's docking area is well-equipped, with walkways leading directly to the beach and main facilities, so visitors can disembark and start enjoying the island right away. The dock is large enough to accommodate Holland America's ships, so getting to the island is hassle-free. It's important to note that because Half Moon Cay is a private island, only passengers on Holland America ships can visit, which means the island never feels overcrowded or overly commercialized.

Getting around Half Moon Cay is simple, as the island is small enough to explore on foot. For those who wish to travel to more distant parts of the island or prefer not to walk, shuttle buses and tram services are available to transport guests to various attractions. The island is accessible for people with disabilities, with wheelchairs available at the dock and several accessible paths throughout the island, though some activities (such as horseback riding) may not be fully accessible.

Operating hours on Half Moon Cay are tied to the cruise ship schedule, with the island typically opening once the ship docks and closing in the late afternoon when it's time for departure. The beach, restaurants, and main attractions are open during these hours, although the island's amenities, such as the water sports rentals and snorkeling tours, may have specific start times depending on the day. It's worth checking with the cruise line for seasonal changes or additional offerings, as the island often runs special events during holidays or peak seasons, such as themed beach parties and live music performances.

For those planning their visit, the best time to visit Half Moon Cay is in the late morning or early afternoon to avoid larger crowds and to take advantage of the full range of activities available. The island is busiest when multiple ships are docked, so it's advisable to check the cruise itinerary ahead of time to determine the busiest days. If you want to avoid the crowds and enjoy a more peaceful experience, try to visit on a day when your ship is one of the few docking at the island.

Safety on Half Moon Cay is a priority, and while the island is generally safe, visitors should still follow basic travel precautions. Stay aware of your belongings, especially on the beach where things like bags and valuables can be left unattended. If you're participating in water activities, always follow the safety guidelines provided by instructors. There are lifeguards on duty in some areas, but it's important to swim only in designated areas to ensure your safety.

For those with disabilities, Half Moon Cay is quite accessible. There are special chairs for use in the water, and the island's transportation options include accessible trams and wheelchairs. It's advisable to contact Holland America Line ahead of time to arrange for specific accommodations, as some areas may be more difficult to access depending on the activity.

One of the hidden gems of Half Moon Cay is its secluded beaches. While the main beach is beautiful, it's worth taking a short walk to the quieter areas of the island where you can enjoy more privacy and perhaps even spot some local wildlife. Additionally, the nature trails on the island offer an opportunity to explore the island's natural beauty away from the crowds.

Half Moon Cay, Bahamas (Holland America Line) offers an exceptional tropical retreat for those looking to escape into paradise. With its mix of adventure, relaxation, and cultural experiences, the island provides something for everyone. Whether you're lounging on the beach, enjoying a horseback ride along the shore, or savoring Bahamian cuisine, Half Moon Cay promises a memorable and tranquil getaway that makes any cruise truly special.

Great Stirrup Cay, Bahamas (Norwegian Cruise Line

Great Stirrup Cay, located in the Bahamas, is a private island exclusively operated by Norwegian Cruise Line (NCL). Situated approximately 120 miles from Nassau in the Berry Islands, this tropical paradise offers a serene and pristine escape for passengers traveling with NCL. The island, which spans about 250 acres, boasts crystal-clear waters, beautiful white-sand beaches, and a variety of activities designed to enhance the cruise experience. Unlike other Bahamian destinations, Great Stirrup Cay remains an exclusive retreat, ensuring guests can experience its beauty in a relatively intimate setting. This private island is not only an ideal spot for relaxation but also offers an array of exciting activities that cater to all types of travelers—from those seeking adventure to those in search of tranquility.

The island is part of the Berry Islands archipelago, which is renowned for its natural beauty, marine life, and quiet charm. Great Stirrup Cay has become a beloved stop for those cruising with Norwegian Cruise Line, known for its low-density tourism, which helps preserve the island's natural beauty while offering an unparalleled experience for visitors. Its accessibility by NCL ships allows passengers to enjoy the best of both worlds: a secluded island retreat with all the amenities and conveniences of a major cruise ship operation.

Visitors to Great Stirrup Cay will find an abundance of activities to enjoy, making it a perfect day stop for adventure seekers and those wishing to unwind. The Beaches are the island's primary attraction, with soft, powdery sand and crystal-clear water. Lighthouse Beach, the most famous, provides a stunning view of the island and the Caribbean Sea. Guests can lounge on the beach, swim in the turquoise waters, or take a leisurely walk along the shoreline. For those looking for more action, there are plenty of watersports and excursions available.

Snorkeling is one of the most popular activities, with vibrant coral reefs just off the coast. Guests can explore these reefs through guided tours, where they might encounter a variety of tropical fish, rays, and even sea turtles. Additionally, kayaking and paddleboarding are popular options for exploring the island's pristine waters. The private cabanas located on the beach provide a more intimate experience, where you can rent a shaded area to relax, enjoy a meal, and have easy access to beach activities.

For thrill-seekers, Great Stirrup Cay offers some unique adventures, including ziplining and paragliding. The zipline takes you high above the island's treetops, providing an exhilarating way to see the lush landscape from a bird's-eye view. Paragliding is another exciting activity, where guests can soar over the waters and enjoy panoramic views of the island. Eco-tours on the island allow visitors to learn about the local flora and fauna, taking in the natural beauty that defines Great Stirrup Cay.

When it comes to dining, visitors will find a variety of restaurants and food options available on the island. The Island Barbecue is a favorite, offering a buffet-style dining experience with fresh local seafood, grilled meats, and tropical fruits. The food is authentic, reflecting the Bahamian flavors that travelers will appreciate during their visit. For a more private experience, guests can reserve a beachfront cabana, where they can enjoy a meal with a stunning view of the ocean and personalized service.

Practical information is crucial for travelers to make the most of their visit. Great Stirrup Cay is designed to cater specifically to NCL guests, with the cruise ships docking directly at the island. The dock is located near the beach, allowing guests to disembark easily and head straight to the attractions. There are no city centers or urban areas nearby, so everything you need is provided on the island, from dining to activities. The transportation around the island is mostly on foot, as Great Stirrup Cay is a small island. However, guests can also take advantage of the tram services that operate between major locations on the island, such as the beach, the cabanas, and the dining areas. There are also plenty of shuttle services available for those with limited mobility.

Great Stirrup Cay's operating hours are tied to the cruise ship schedule. The island is typically open from the moment the ship docks until its departure in the late afternoon. The main attractions, such as the beach, water sports, and dining facilities, are available during these hours. The island is most vibrant during the high cruise season, which runs from December to April. However, due to its exclusivity, it never feels overcrowded, even during peak periods. For those looking for a quieter experience, it is best to visit on weekdays when fewer ships are scheduled to dock.

For travelers looking to avoid crowds, visiting the island early in the day or later in the afternoon is a great strategy. Safety tips on Great Stirrup Cay include remaining cautious of your personal belongings, especially when swimming or participating in beach activities. It's also recommended to stay within designated swimming areas to ensure your safety, as currents can be strong outside these zones. As with any beach destination, it's important to stay hydrated and use sunscreen, as the sun can be quite intense, especially during the summer months.

Great Stirrup Cay offers accessibility features for guests with disabilities. Accessible paths and beach access are available, and there are also beach wheelchairs for use. For guests with mobility concerns, it's a good idea to contact Norwegian Cruise Line ahead of time to arrange for any specific needs, as not all areas may be fully accessible for those with limited mobility.

One of the hidden gems of Great Stirrup Cay is the secluded coves around the island. These quieter areas offer a perfect opportunity for those looking for a more private and peaceful beach experience. You might even find yourself enjoying a moment of solitude in an area where you can hear only the sounds of the ocean and feel the gentle breeze.

Great Stirrup Cay, Bahamas, offers a perfect balance of relaxation, adventure, and cultural richness for Norwegian Cruise Line passengers. Whether you're looking to relax on pristine beaches, experience Bahamian cuisine, or take part in thrilling activities, this private island has something for everyone.

Amber Cove, Dominican Republic (Carnival)

Amber Cove, located on the northern coast of the Dominican Republic, is a vibrant and relatively new cruise port operated by Carnival Corporation. Situated in the Puerto Plata region, Amber Cove serves as a gateway to the country's rich culture, natural beauty, and historical significance. As part of the Amber Coast, the area is named after the fossilized tree resin that is abundant in the region, which once played a crucial role in the country's economy. For travelers arriving at this port, Amber Cove offers an ideal mix of relaxation, adventure, and cultural immersion, making it an increasingly popular stop for cruise passengers.

The Dominican Republic is known for its deep-rooted cultural diversity, with influences from Taino, African, and European cultures. Amber Cove itself has been developed to offer visitors a glimpse of this dynamic heritage while integrating modern amenities and attractions to cater to international visitors. What makes Amber Cove stand out is its ability to blend the natural beauty of the region with the welcoming spirit of its people, ensuring a memorable stop for cruise-goers.

Amber Cove's history is closely linked to the Amber Coast, known for the amber deposits found along its shores. Amber has been a symbol of the region's natural wealth for centuries, with the Dominican Republic being one of the world's largest producers of this ancient resin. The amber industry, once a major source of income for the country, continues to influence the economy and culture of the area. Historically, the region was home to the Taino people, the island's indigenous inhabitants, who used amber in various cultural and spiritual practices.

The town of Puerto Plata, not far from Amber Cove, also has significant historical importance. Founded in the late 15th century, it was one of the first European settlements in the Americas. The Fortaleza San Felipe, an old Spanish fort, stands as a reminder of the island's colonial past and its defense against pirates. The port of Amber Cove is located near Puerto Plata, making it easy for visitors to explore these historical landmarks and gain deeper insights into the region's colonial history.

Key Attractions and Activities

Amber Cove is designed to offer a comprehensive experience for cruise passengers, combining relaxation, adventure, and cultural exposure. Here are some of the key attractions and activities at the port:

1. Amber Cove Port Complex: The port itself is a hub of activity, featuring a wide range of shops, restaurants, and

leisure facilities. It's an excellent starting point for exploring the region, with its swimming pools, jacuzzi, and lush landscaping. The Amber Cove Waterpark is especially popular, offering fun slides and a lazy river for families and thrill-seekers alike.

2. Historic Puerto Plata: Located just a short distance from the port, Puerto Plata is a town steeped in history. A visit to Fortaleza San Felipe, a 16th-century fort, offers visitors a glimpse into the past. The Museo del Ámbar (Amber Museum) is also a must-see, showcasing the rich history of amber mining in the region and the unique specimens found here, some of which contain ancient fossils.

3. Cable Car Ride to Mount Isabel de Torres: For breathtaking views, a ride on the Puerto Plata Cable Car is an unforgettable experience. It takes visitors from the city up to Mount Isabel de Torres, where a large statue of Christ the Redeemer overlooks the town. At the top, there are lush gardens and panoramic views of the city, the coastline, and the surrounding mountains.

4. Beaches and Water Activities: Amber Cove is surrounded by natural beauty, including some gorgeous beaches. Playa Dorada is a popular beach close to the port, offering clear waters and a range of water sports, such as snorkeling, scuba diving, and kayaking. Those seeking a more secluded beach experience can explore Cofresi Beach, a quieter and less commercialized spot.

5. Excursions to the Damajagua Waterfalls: For more adventurous visitors, the Damajagua Waterfalls are a must-see. A short drive from Amber Cove, this series of 27

waterfalls is a popular destination for hiking and waterfall jumping. You can explore the falls by foot, and for those who are up for it, jumping into the natural pools below is an exhilarating experience.

Local Cuisine and Dining Options
Amber Cove and Puerto Plata offer a taste of traditional Dominican cuisine, rich in flavors and locally sourced ingredients. For a more authentic experience, visitors can try mangu, a dish made of mashed plantains, often served with eggs and salami. Mofongo, made from fried plantains and garlic, is another delicious local dish. For seafood lovers, pescado frito (fried fish) and lobster are popular choices.

While there are several dining options within the Amber Cove port complex, some local spots in Puerto Plata offer more traditional Dominican meals. La Diligencia is a well-known restaurant that serves up fresh seafood and regional dishes in a casual setting. For a more upscale experience, Los Pescadores in Puerto Plata provides delicious seafood with a view of the ocean.

Practical Information for Travelers Visiting Amber Cove, Dominican Republic (Carnival)
Cruise ships visiting Amber Cove dock directly at the port's modern terminal. The port is well-equipped with amenities like shopping centers, restaurants, and even a swimming pool. It's located about 15 minutes from the heart of Puerto Plata, making it easy for visitors to venture into the town for sightseeing or shopping.

Transportation Options

While you can easily explore Amber Cove by walking around the port area, those who wish to travel beyond the complex can rely on taxis, private tours, or shuttle buses. Taxis are available at the port, though it's recommended to negotiate fares in advance or use ride-hailing apps if available. Private excursions are also a great way to see more of the region, with many tour operators offering trips to local attractions such as the waterfalls or cable car ride.

For those looking to explore the nearby beaches or historical sites, shuttle services from the port can take you to places like Playa Dorada and Puerto Plata. Public transportation options are available but may be less convenient for tourists who are unfamiliar with the area.

Operating Hours and Seasonal Considerations

Amber Cove is open when cruise ships dock, typically from morning to late afternoon. The best time to visit is between November and April, which offers the most favorable weather conditions—warm temperatures and little rain. However, the Dominican Republic is a tropical destination, so brief rain showers are possible year-round.

Visitor Tips for Amber Cove, Dominican Republic (Carnival)

Best Times to Visit

To avoid the crowds, it's ideal to visit popular attractions early in the day, especially the Cable Car and the Damajagua Waterfalls, which can become crowded later in the day. Visiting in the morning also gives you more time to relax at the beach or explore Puerto Plata.

Safety Tips

While Amber Cove is generally safe, it's wise to stay aware of your surroundings, especially when leaving the port area. Stick to well-populated areas and avoid venturing too far from established tourist routes. Always use reputable taxi services and agree on the fare before departure.

Amber Cove and Puerto Plata have made strides to accommodate travelers with disabilities, with wheelchair-accessible transport available for certain excursions. However, some natural attractions, such as the Damajagua Waterfalls, may be challenging for those with limited mobility due to uneven terrain and steep paths.

Local Insights and Hidden Gems
For a deeper dive into Dominican culture, consider a visit to Puerto Plata's Central Park, where you can experience the local vibe. A stop at the Amber Museum offers a fascinating look at the region's unique geological history, with amber pieces dating back millions of years.

Cultural events, such as the Merengue Festival in Puerto Plata (typically held in July), offer a wonderful opportunity to experience Dominican music and dance traditions.

Amber Cove, Dominican Republic, is more than just a stop on a cruise—it's an immersive destination offering a blend of natural beauty, rich history, and vibrant culture. Whether you're seeking adventure at the waterfalls, relaxing on stunning beaches, or exploring the historical town of Puerto Plata, Amber Cove has something for everyone. By exploring the lesser-known attractions and embracing the local culture, visitors will have a truly memorable experience that goes beyond the usual tourist trail.

CHAPTER 7.
EXCURSION AND ADVENTURES

Snorkeling and Diving Highlights

Snorkeling and diving in the Caribbean are more than just water activities; they are gateways to an underwater paradise teeming with vibrant life and stunning seascapes. The region's crystal-clear waters, warm temperatures, and unparalleled marine biodiversity make it one of the world's most sought-after destinations for exploring beneath the waves. From shallow coral gardens to dramatic underwater walls, the Caribbean offers something for every level of snorkeler and diver.

Among the top destinations for underwater exploration, Grand Cayman stands out with its famous Stingray City and the vibrant coral formations at Devil's Grotto. The waters around Cozumel, Mexico, draw divers and snorkelers from across the globe, with Palancar Reef offering a kaleidoscope of colors and abundant sea life. Bonaire, often called a diver's paradise, is celebrated for its pristine reefs and easy shore diving. In the Bahamas, the Exuma Cays promise surreal encounters with nurse sharks and the famous Thunderball Grotto, while the U.S. Virgin Islands offer secluded bays like Trunk Bay in St. John, perfect for beginner snorkelers. San Juan in Puerto Rico also provides access to captivating underwater environments such as the vibrant coral reefs around Vieques.

The marine life in these destinations is as enchanting as the scenery itself. Brightly colored parrotfish, angelfish, and butterflyfish glide gracefully around intricate coral formations. Green sea turtles and hawksbill turtles are a common sight in places like Akumal, Mexico, while eagle rays and gentle nurse sharks can often be spotted gliding in the distance. More adventurous divers might encounter Caribbean reef sharks or explore wreck sites where marine life thrives in artificial habitats. The coral gardens, alive with soft and hard corals, create a mesmerizing underwater landscape, offering a feast for the senses and plenty of photo opportunities.

For cruise passengers, snorkeling and diving excursions are widely available and cater to a variety of skill levels. Beginners can opt for guided snorkeling tours that provide equipment and instruction, making it easy to explore vibrant reefs just below the surface. Experienced divers can choose more advanced excursions, including wall dives, wreck dives, and night dives that unveil a completely different side of the underwater world. Many ports offer convenient rentals for gear, and professional operators often organize half-day or full-day trips to prime locations, ensuring travelers maximize their time.

Safety is paramount for these activities, and travelers should always choose reputable operators with strong safety records. Checking reviews and certifications like PADI for dive shops can ensure a positive experience. Understanding local conditions, such as currents and water visibility, is also important, particularly for independent snorkelers or divers. For those new to snorkeling, wearing a life vest can provide added confidence. Additionally, respecting the marine environment is essential; avoid touching coral reefs, as they are fragile ecosystems, and use reef-safe sunscreen to minimize impact on aquatic life.

Snorkeling and diving are must-do activities for anyone visiting the Caribbean. These experiences offer a chance to connect with the ocean in ways that few other activities can, revealing an underwater realm that feels like another planet. Whether you're floating on the surface or descending into the depths, the magic of the Caribbean's marine life will stay with you long after you return to shore.

Nature and Wildlife Encounters

The Caribbean is a treasure trove of natural wonders and vibrant wildlife, where lush rainforests, shimmering coral reefs, and tranquil mangroves come together to create a haven for biodiversity. These unique ecosystems form the heart of the region, supporting a dazzling variety of life both above and below the waterline. The region's tropical rainforests are alive with the calls of exotic birds and the rustle of foliage as curious iguanas and other creatures move about. Coastal mangroves act as nurseries for marine life and provide shelter for countless bird species, while coral reefs teem with color and motion, offering a spectacle of nature that is both mesmerizing and fragile.

For travelers seeking intimate wildlife encounters, certain destinations within the Caribbean stand out as unparalleled. The Cayman Islands, known for their tranquil waters, are perfect for spotting stingrays gliding gracefully through the sandbanks of Stingray City. The Tobago Cays Marine Park offers a breathtaking setting to swim alongside green sea turtles as they graze on seagrass meadows. St. Lucia's lush landscapes provide the chance to see its famous St. Lucia parrot, an endemic species that thrives in the island's dense forests. Bonaire, a leader in conservation, is a paradise for birdwatchers and divers alike, with its flamingos and pristine underwater world. Puerto Rico's El Yunque National Forest invites visitors to explore its verdant trails, where coquí frogs and vibrant tropical flowers make every step a discovery.

Underwater, the Caribbean is alive with marine creatures that seem to dance to the rhythm of the tides. Dolphins often accompany boats, leaping playfully in the surf, while manta rays glide silently through the depths like underwater kites. Schools of tropical fish, their scales shimmering in hues of blue, yellow, and red, flit between coral structures that appear sculpted by nature's hand. Specific sites such as Cozumel's Palancar Reef and the reefs of the Bahamas offer thrilling encounters for snorkelers and divers, who may also catch sight of nurse sharks resting in sandy coves or even the occasional whale shark during migration seasons.

On land, the region's wildlife is equally captivating. In the Dominican Republic, visitors can join eco-tours to observe the critically endangered rhinoceros iguana in its natural habitat. The wetlands of Trinidad and Tobago are home to the Scarlet Ibis, whose vivid plumage turns the sky into a canvas of red at dusk. Guided hikes in the Virgin Islands reveal the region's smaller wonders, from tiny hummingbirds darting among flowers to the mesmerizing patterns of a hermit crab inching across the sand. These encounters provide a sense of connection to the land that few other activities can offer.

The Caribbean's dedication to conservation is evident in the efforts of local organizations and global partnerships working to preserve its natural treasures. From sea turtle nesting programs to coral restoration projects, these initiatives highlight the region's commitment to sustainability. Travelers can contribute by participating in eco-tours, supporting local conservation organizations, or simply adhering to responsible tourism practices, such as avoiding single-use plastics and respecting wildlife guidelines.

For cruise passengers, excursions centered on nature and wildlife offer unique and enriching experiences. Options range from tranquil birdwatching tours to thrilling wildlife safaris that explore remote corners of the islands. Guided kayaking trips through mangrove forests provide an up-close view of these vital ecosystems, while snorkeling expeditions reveal the vibrant underwater world just beneath the surface. These excursions are often led by knowledgeable guides who share insights about the region's ecology, making each journey both educational and unforgettable.

Interacting with wildlife requires care and respect. Observing animals from a safe distance ensures their natural behaviors remain undisturbed, while following guidelines from tour operators helps protect fragile ecosystems. you should avoid feeding wildlife or attempting physical interactions, as these can disrupt the delicate balance of their environments.

Wearing reef-safe sunscreen and minimizing waste are simple yet impactful ways to contribute to the health of these habitats.

Nature and wildlife encounters in the Caribbean offer more than just moments of wonder; they provide a deeper understanding of the region's extraordinary beauty and diversity. From the vibrant coral reefs to the song-filled rainforests, these experiences invite travelers to connect with the world in profound and meaningful ways. For anyone visiting the Caribbean, they are not just an option but an essential part of the journey.

Adventure Activities: Zip-lining, ATVs, and Hiking

Adventure in the Caribbean is something you don't want to miss. Imagine yourself flying through the air on a zip-line, the rainforest rushing past in a blur of green as you take in views that feel almost unreal. Or maybe you'd rather hop on an ATV, kicking up a trail of dust as you navigate rugged paths that lead to hidden beaches or ancient ruins. If you're like me and enjoy slowing down to soak in your surroundings, hiking might be your thing—trekking through lush forests to discover waterfalls, exotic wildlife, or sweeping panoramic views. Trust me, these experiences will add a whole new dimension to your cruise vacation.

Let's talk about zip-lining first. Picture yourself in Puerto Rico, gliding high above the treetops of El Yunque Rainforest. The thrill of launching off the platform mixes with the serenity of soaring over such incredible scenery. If you're headed to St. Lucia, zip-lining there gives you a chance to take in views of the iconic Pitons while feeling the rush of wind in your face. And Jamaica? The Mystic Mountain park takes it up a notch with views of the coastline you won't soon forget. I'd recommend sticking with reputable operators like Rainforest Adventures or Toro Verde—they make safety a top priority, and their guides are not only skilled but also make the experience so much fun. Oh, and don't forget to wear comfy clothes and shoes that won't slip off mid-flight!

Now, if the idea of getting off the beaten path appeals to you, ATV tours are where it's at. Riding an ATV is such a fun way to explore the island landscapes up close. I loved zipping through Cozumel's jungle paths, where the scent of the tropical air mixes with the excitement of the ride. Over in the Dominican Republic, you'll find trails that wind through rolling hills and sugarcane fields, often ending at a beautiful river or secluded beach. And if you're in Aruba, the desert-like terrain offers a completely different vibe, with rugged trails leading to natural wonders like limestone caves or dramatic cliffs. The key to a great ride is picking an operator that knows their stuff. Operators like Wild Tours in Cozumel or Rancho Loco in Aruba offer well-maintained vehicles and guides who know how to make the trip safe and exciting. Pro tip: wear long pants and shoes that'll stay put—your legs will thank you after a day of adventuring.

If you prefer something a little slower-paced but just as rewarding, hiking is the way to go. There's nothing quite like walking through Puerto Rico's El Yunque Rainforest, where the air feels fresh and cool under the dense canopy, and the sound of waterfalls grows louder with each step. Dominica is another hiker's dream—it's known as the "Nature Isle" for good reason. Trails here lead to incredible sights like the steaming Boiling Lake or Trafalgar Falls. I still remember hiking up Gros Piton in St. Lucia; the climb was challenging, but the view from the top made every step worth it. Whether you choose a guided tour or decide to explore on your own, be sure to pack plenty of water, sturdy shoes, and maybe a snack or two. You'll want to stay energized for those unforgettable moments along the trail.

And hey, why not combine these activities? Start your morning zip-lining through the trees, then jump on an ATV to explore nearby trails, and cap off the day with a peaceful hike to a waterfall. It's like getting three adventures in one day—and believe me, you'll feel like you've truly made the most of your time.

Adventure activities like these aren't just about the rush; they're about seeing the Caribbean in a way that most people don't. You'll discover the islands' raw, natural beauty and feel connected to the landscapes in a way that's hard to put into words.

CHAPTER 8.
BEACH BLISS
Best Beaches by Region

The beaches of the Caribbean have a magic all their own. Just imagine soft sands under your feet, waves rolling gently to shore, and water so clear you can see every shell and fish beneath the surface. Whether you're dreaming of peaceful moments with a good book or exciting adventures in the surf, these beaches are the perfect escape. Each region has its own personality, offering a mix of lively vibes and tranquil retreats. Let me walk you through some of the very best spots to dip your toes in the sand and lose track of time.

In the Eastern Caribbean, you'll find beaches that look like they've come straight out of a postcard. Magens Bay in St. Thomas is one of those places that feels almost too perfect to be real. The water is calm and inviting, making it a great spot for swimming. If you're more into exploring, Trunk Bay in St. John has an underwater snorkeling trail that's perfect for discovering colorful marine life just below the surface. The vibe is a little quieter, ideal for soaking up nature's beauty. Over on St. Maarten, Orient Beach is where you'll want to go if you're in the mood for lively energy. There are beach bars, water sports, and a social scene that's hard to beat. Each of these beaches has something special, and it's worth spending time to see what makes them unique.

The Western Caribbean has its own gems. Seven Mile Beach in Grand Cayman is a long, dreamy stretch of sand where you can wander for what feels like forever. The turquoise water is so clear that snorkeling becomes an absolute must—you might even spot a stingray or two. In Jamaica, Doctor's Cave Beach has a rich history and a fun, welcoming atmosphere. The water is known for its mineral content, and some even say it has healing properties. Pair that with easy access to local jerk chicken spots, and you've got a day to remember. If you're stopping in Mexico, Playa del Carmen offers a vibrant mix of beachfront relaxation and nearby adventures. You can sunbathe, snorkel, or take a quick trip to explore Mayan ruins.

The Southern Caribbean feels like a different world entirely. Aruba's Eagle Beach is a slice of paradise with its iconic divi-divi trees and soft, powdery sand. It's the kind of place where time just seems to slow down. Dickenson Bay in Antigua is another favorite, offering calm waters and a perfect setting for paddleboarding or just floating aimlessly in the sea. For something a little more off the beaten path, head to Pinney's Beach in Nevis. It's laid-back and peaceful, with views of the mountains adding a stunning backdrop. There's often a local vendor grilling fresh seafood right on the beach, and trust me, it's something you won't want to miss.

One of the best parts about these beaches is the variety of activities and amenities they offer. If you love snorkeling, many of these beaches are surrounded by reefs teeming with life. Paddleboarding is another great way to explore the water if you prefer staying above the surface. For a more relaxed vibe, there are plenty of spots with beach bars serving up tropical drinks. And the little conveniences like clean restrooms, rental chairs, or shady cabanas can make a world of difference for a comfortable day by the sea.

A few tips can help you make the most of your beach day. The earlier you arrive, the better—especially at popular spots like Seven Mile Beach or Magens Bay. Morning light is gorgeous for photos, and you'll beat the crowds for a peaceful start. It's always a good idea to check how far the beach is from your cruise port and plan transportation in advance. Some places offer shuttles, while others might need a taxi or short hike. And remember to respect local customs—some beaches have areas designated for specific activities or even clothing-optional sections, so it's worth doing a little homework beforehand.

Every one of these beaches is a slice of paradise in its own way. They offer not just relaxation but a chance to connect with the natural beauty of the Caribbean. I know I've made some of my best cruise memories with my toes in the sand and a view of endless blue in front of me. So take a deep breath, embrace the slower pace of island time, and let yourself fully enjoy the beauty of these stunning shores. It's your time to soak up the sun and create moments you'll never forget.

Secluded vs. Popular Beaches

When planning a trip to the Caribbean, one of the most exciting decisions you'll make is choosing which beaches to visit. The islands offer everything from lively, bustling shores with every amenity imaginable to peaceful, hidden gems where the only sounds are the gentle lapping of waves and the rustle of palm trees. Deciding between secluded and popular beaches is a matter of preference, but both types offer their own charm and unique experiences.

Popular beaches are often the heart of activity. Places like Seven Mile Beach in Jamaica or Eagle Beach in Aruba are known worldwide for their stunning beauty and convenient facilities. These beaches tend to have soft, golden sands, clear waters, and an atmosphere buzzing with energy. Vendors selling refreshing coconuts, opportunities to try water sports like parasailing or jet skiing, and beach bars serving colorful cocktails make these destinations perfect for those seeking a lively and social experience. Families, in particular, might enjoy the conveniences of these spots, as there are often lifeguards, restrooms, and nearby restaurants to ensure everyone's comfort.

On the other hand, these popular beaches can sometimes feel crowded, especially during peak tourist seasons. The hustle and bustle might take away from the serenity you might be craving, and finding a quiet spot to relax can be a challenge. Still, for travelers who thrive on vibrant surroundings and enjoy meeting fellow beachgoers from around the world, these beaches are an excellent choice.

Secluded beaches, however, are where the magic of solitude truly shines. Picture yourself on a remote stretch of sand like Anse La Roche in Grenada or Little Bay Beach in Anguilla. These hidden treasures are often more difficult to access, requiring a hike, a boat ride, or guidance from locals who know the best-kept secrets of the area. But the effort is well worth it. These beaches are havens of tranquility, where you might have the shoreline almost entirely to yourself. The feeling of isolation, paired with the pristine surroundings, creates an atmosphere that's as close to paradise as you can imagine.

Secluded beaches are ideal for couples seeking romance, solo travelers looking to connect with nature, or anyone wanting to escape the noise of everyday life. You can lie on the sand undisturbed, listen to the waves, and let time drift away. Without the distractions of vendors or crowded activities, you'll find it easier to appreciate the natural beauty of your surroundings – from the soft whisper of the breeze to the shimmer of the water under the sun.

However, it's essential to come prepared when visiting these hidden spots. Secluded beaches often lack facilities, so bringing your own snacks, water, sunscreen, and a towel is a must. Safety is another consideration – always inform someone of your plans if you're heading to a remote area, and be cautious of strong currents if lifeguards aren't present.

For those who can't decide, a mix of both types of beaches can offer the best of both worlds. Spend a day at a popular beach enjoying the buzz and excitement, then retreat to a quieter shore for some peace and solitude. This way, you can experience the full spectrum of what the Caribbean's coastline has to offer.

Whether you choose the lively charm of popular beaches or the serene beauty of secluded ones, the Caribbean has no shortage of stunning options. Each beach, with its own personality and allure, adds a unique touch to your journey. From vibrant sunsets over a crowded shore to quiet moments of reflection on a deserted stretch of sand, your time by the sea will surely leave lasting memories. The choice is yours – dive into the energy or sink into the calm, or better yet, try a little of both.

Tips for a Perfect Beach Day

A perfect beach day can be one of the most relaxing and enjoyable experiences, but a little preparation can make it even better. Whether you're visiting a well-known beach or a hidden gem, there are a few simple tips that can help you make the most of your time by the sea.

First, it's important to choose the right beach for the experience you want. If you're looking for calm waters and a quiet atmosphere, beaches like Bavaro Beach in Punta Cana or Bahia de las Aguilas in the southwest offer serene environments perfect for swimming and relaxing. If you're looking for more action, Playa Dorada in Puerto Plata offers water sports and a lively beach scene. Once you've picked your spot, it's time to pack the essentials.

Start with sunscreen. Even on cloudy days, the sun's rays can still cause damage, so it's crucial to apply sunscreen generously and often throughout the day. A high SPF, water-resistant sunscreen is a great choice for extended beach days. Make sure to cover all areas of exposed skin, including your back, shoulders, and feet. It's always a good idea to have a hat and sunglasses to protect your face and eyes, especially in the afternoon when the sun is stronger.

Next, bring enough water to stay hydrated. Spending hours in the sun can quickly leave you feeling thirsty, so it's important to drink plenty of water to avoid dehydration. You can also pack some snacks like fruit, nuts, or granola bars to keep your energy up. If you're planning to stay for several hours, having a cooler with refreshments is a smart move.

If you want to enjoy the beach comfortably, bringing a good beach towel or blanket is key. Look for one that's large enough to spread out on the sand but not so heavy that it's hard to carry. A beach chair or portable lounger can also make a big difference for long days by the water. If you're planning to lay in the sun, consider an umbrella or a pop-up tent to create some shade. This will help protect you from the sun and give you a cool place to retreat to when you need a break.

Don't forget about beach footwear. Sand can get hot, so flip-flops or water shoes are essential for walking to and from the water. If you plan on swimming, water shoes can also protect your feet from sharp rocks or coral under the surface.

While you're on the beach, take the time to relax and enjoy the surroundings. Whether you're reading a book, taking a nap, or simply watching the waves, the beach is the perfect place to unwind. If you enjoy water activities, consider renting a paddleboard, kayak, or snorkeling gear. Many beaches offer rentals for these activities, and it's a great way to explore the water.

If you're in the mood for a swim, remember to always check the water conditions. Some beaches may have strong currents or waves, so it's important to swim in areas that are marked as safe. Always follow lifeguard instructions and be mindful of your surroundings.

For an extra fun experience, bring a beach ball, frisbee, or volleyball to play with friends or family. It's a great way to stay active while enjoying the fresh air. Some beaches even offer beach volleyball courts or other organized games, so check out what's available.

As the day winds down, don't forget to take some time to watch the sunset. Many beaches offer stunning sunset views that make the end of the day feel extra special. Whether you're enjoying a cocktail, taking pictures, or just relaxing, it's a perfect way to wrap up a perfect beach day.

When you're getting ready to leave, remember to clean up after yourself. Take all your trash with you, and if possible, dispose of it in recycling bins to help keep the beach beautiful for others. Leave the sand as you found it so everyone can enjoy the beach as much as you did.

Overall, a perfect beach day is about taking it easy and enjoying the beauty of nature. With a little preparation and the right attitude, it can be a memorable experience filled with relaxation, fun, and stunning views. So, pack your bag, grab your sunscreen, and head to the beach—it's time to enjoy the sun and the sea.

CHAPTER 9.
CULINARY DELIGHTS
Iconic Caribbean Dishes to Try

Caribbean cuisine is a celebration of bold flavors, vibrant colors, and deep cultural traditions. Each bite tells a story of the region's rich history, blending indigenous, African, European, and Indian influences into dishes that are as diverse as the islands themselves. The magic of Caribbean food lies in its five distinct flavors: the warmth of spices, the tang of citrus, the sweetness of tropical fruits, the umami of fresh seafood, and the earthiness of root vegetables. These flavors form the heart of the Caribbean's culinary identity, and each offers a unique taste of the islands' spirit.

The warmth of spices is unmistakable in dishes like jerk chicken or pork, especially in Jamaica. Jerk seasoning is a fiery blend of allspice, Scotch bonnet peppers, thyme, and cinnamon, giving the meat a smoky, sweet, and spicy flavor when grilled over pimento wood. It's a must-try for those who crave a little heat with their meals. For those with allergies or dietary restrictions, such as sensitivity to peppers, ask the chef if the spice level can be adjusted—Caribbean chefs are often happy to tailor their creations.

The tang of citrus is another defining note in Caribbean cuisine, especially in marinades and sauces. Lime and orange juice are key players, brightening up dishes like ceviche or grilled fish. In Trinidad and Tobago, citrus is also used in condiments like pepper sauce, where lime juice balances the heat. If you're avoiding high-acid foods, opt for citrus-infused beverages like limeade, which lets you enjoy the flavor without the intensity.

The sweetness of tropical fruits is a joy in the Caribbean. Think ripe mangoes, pineapples, and guavas, often served fresh or as the base for desserts and sauces. In Barbados, flying fish with a sweet mango chutney is a national treasure. For those with sugar sensitivities, these fruits offer a natural alternative to refined sugars in desserts and smoothies. Just confirm with your server that no additional sweeteners are added.

The umami of fresh seafood is a staple in island kitchens, where fish, shrimp, and lobster come straight from the sea. Dishes like St. Lucian bouillabaisse or Bahamian conch salad showcase the incredible quality of the seafood here. If you have shellfish allergies, don't worry—many menus feature non-seafood options with equally bold flavors, such as plantain-based dishes or vegetable curries.

Finally, the earthiness of root vegetables anchors many Caribbean meals. Yams, sweet potatoes, cassava, and breadfruit are often roasted, fried, or mashed. In Puerto Rico, mofongo—a dish made from mashed plantains with garlic and pork cracklings—is a delicious example. For gluten-free travelers, these starchy roots provide a safe and satisfying option. Just ask about preparation methods to ensure they meet your dietary needs, as some recipes might include dairy or cross-contamination in frying oils.

To safely enjoy these vibrant flavors, let your servers know about any allergies or restrictions upfront. Many Caribbean chefs are skilled at adapting dishes to accommodate their guests, and menus often highlight allergen-friendly options. Be adventurous, try new dishes, and savor the experience, knowing there's something delicious for every palate.

Rum and Local Drinks Guide

Rum and the Caribbean go hand in hand, don't they? It's more than just a drink here—it's a piece of history, a symbol of celebration, and a true taste of the islands. From the days of sugar plantations to the vibrant beach bars you'll stumble upon today, rum is deeply woven into the culture. Every sip tells a story, and trust me, exploring the world of Caribbean rum is one of the most enjoyable ways to connect with the spirit of this region.

If you're heading to Jamaica, you're in for a treat. The rum here has a boldness to it that's just unmistakable. Appleton Estate is one of the most iconic names, and their rums are rich, complex, and perfect for sipping or mixing. You can't leave without trying a classic Jamaican Rum Punch. It's fruity, sweet, and spiced just right—a true island favorite. Or, for something with a little ginger kick, a Jamaican Mule is refreshing and pairs beautifully with the tropical heat.

Barbados has a rum heritage that's hard to beat. Mount Gay Rum, often referred to as the world's oldest rum brand, is a must-try. It's smooth and flavorful, and the distillery offers fascinating tours if you're curious about the craft behind the drink. While you're there, order a Barbados Rum Sour. It's a perfectly balanced cocktail that feels like sunshine in a glass, with hints of citrus and sweetness blending seamlessly with the rum's character.

In Puerto Rico, the rum culture is as lively as the island itself. Bacardi is a name you'll recognize, and their distillery tour is a fun way to dive into the process of making rum. Puerto Rico is also the birthplace of the Piña Colada, and I promise, the creamy mix of rum, pineapple, and coconut tastes better here than anywhere else. If you're in the mood for something lighter, a Mojito made with fresh mint and lime is a refreshing pick.

St. Lucia's rum scene is equally impressive. Chairman's Reserve is a local gem, known for its smooth and aromatic profile. It's a fantastic choice for sipping neat or in cocktails. The island also has a knack for creative twists, so don't be surprised if you come across innovative rum drinks with local fruits and spices.

Of course, rum isn't the only drink worth trying in the Caribbean. Fresh tropical juices are everywhere, and they're as vibrant as the scenery. Guava, passionfruit, and tamarind juices are like tasting the islands in liquid form. If you're a beer lover, Red Stripe from Jamaica and Presidente from the Dominican Republic are excellent local brews to pair with a day at the beach. And don't forget about the refreshing simplicity of coconut water straight from the shell—hydrating, sweet, and absolutely delicious.

Finding the perfect spot to enjoy these drinks is part of the adventure. Beach bars are always a good idea, offering not just great drinks but unforgettable views and laid-back vibes. Look out for smaller shacks or roadside stands—they often have the most authentic flavors and some of the friendliest people you'll meet. In cruise ports, ask locals where they go for a drink. They'll often point you to a hidden gem you'd never find on your own.

One thing I've learned is that drinking in the Caribbean is as much about the experience as it is about the flavors. There's often a toast involved—"cheers" here might sound like "salud" or "to life," depending on where you are. It's all about taking a moment to celebrate good company and the beauty around you. Some places even have unique traditions, like clinking glasses before the first sip or making a toast to the sea.

Exploring rum and local drinks is like tasting the soul of the Caribbean. Each sip has a way of bringing the islands closer to you, with flavors that linger long after your trip ends.

Best Local Restaurants Near Ports

Exploring local eateries near ports is a wonderful way to experience the authentic flavors of a region. Whether you're looking for an upscale dining experience, a cozy hideaway, or a farm-to-table restaurant showcasing regional ingredients, there's something for everyone. Here's a list of must-try restaurants near popular ports, each with its own special vibe and menu.

1. The Cliff (Barbados)
- Atmosphere: The Cliff is a romantic, upscale restaurant offering stunning views of the Caribbean Sea. Set on a cliffside, the ambiance is elegant with soft lighting, cozy outdoor seating, and a calm, intimate atmosphere. It's perfect for a special evening with a loved one.
- Pricing: Expect a higher-end price range, with appetizers starting around $20 USD, main courses from $40 to $60 USD, and desserts around $15 USD.
- Signature Dishes: The signature dish here is the Grilled Lobster served with a citrus beurre blanc sauce. It's fresh, flavorful, and captures the essence of local seafood. They also serve a Lamb Rack, which is beautifully seasoned and tender.

2. Oistins Fish Fry (Barbados)
- Atmosphere: A more casual, laid-back spot, Oistins is a must-visit for those who want to experience local culture. Located by the water in Oistins, this vibrant fish fry area is filled with local vendors offering fresh seafood, music, and a relaxed vibe.
- Pricing: Affordable, with meals typically ranging from $10 to $20 USD. Most dishes are served in generous portions, offering great value.
- Signature Dishes: Don't miss the Grilled Flying Fish, which is a staple in Barbados. Served with rice and peas, it's a delicious and satisfying local meal. Another local favorite is Bajan Pepperpot, a slow-cooked stew made with beef, pork, and vegetables in a rich, spicy broth.

3. Café des Arts (Martinique)

- Atmosphere: Café des Arts offers a warm, cozy atmosphere with a mix of contemporary and traditional French-Caribbean design. It's casual enough for a laid-back lunch but elegant enough for a romantic dinner. Situated in Fort-de-France, the restaurant offers a scenic view of the waterfront.
- Pricing: Mid-range pricing. Expect appetizers starting around $12 USD, main dishes from $20 to $30 USD, and desserts at around $10 USD.
- Signature Dishes: The Grilled Tuna Steak is a standout, often served with a side of sweet plantains and local vegetables. You can also try the Creole Bouillabaisse, a seafood stew made with fresh catches from the Caribbean Sea.

4. The Fish Pot (Barbados)
- Atmosphere: This restaurant, located on the water's edge in the charming village of Inch Marlowe, offers a more relaxed but intimate setting with casual beach-style decor and a peaceful, cozy atmosphere. It's perfect for a quiet meal while enjoying a view of the ocean.
- Pricing: Moderate. Appetizers cost between $10 to $20 USD, mains between $25 to $40 USD, and desserts from $10 to $15 USD.
- Signature Dishes: Try their Pan-Seared Snapper, which is served with a tangy, herbaceous sauce that complements the fresh fish. The Jamaican Jerk Lobster is also a popular option, cooked perfectly with smoky, spicy flavors.

5. La Table de Mamy Nounou (Guadeloupe)
- Atmosphere: This charming, family-run restaurant in the heart of Guadeloupe exudes a welcoming and homey feel. The atmosphere is casual yet warm, perfect for families or anyone

looking for a traditional Caribbean meal with a twist. The rustic interior adds to its cozy ambiance.
- Pricing: Very affordable, with appetizers ranging from $7 to $12 USD, mains from $15 to $25 USD, and desserts for around $6 to $10 USD.
- Signature Dishes: The Poulet Boucané (smoked chicken) is a must-try dish. It's cooked slowly to retain its smoky flavor, complemented by a tangy local sauce. Their Accras de Morue (cod fritters) are also very popular and are a great starter.

6. La Creole (St. Lucia)
- Atmosphere: Situated near the port in Castries, La Creole has a relaxed yet elegant vibe. The outdoor seating area offers a great view of the harbor, making it perfect for a casual, breezy meal while watching the boats come and go. It's a great place to unwind after a day of exploration.
- Pricing: Moderate pricing. Expect appetizers around $12 to $18 USD, mains between $20 to $35 USD, and desserts around $8 to $12 USD.
- Signature Dishes: The Creole Seafood Platter is a popular choice, featuring lobster, shrimp, and fish in a rich, spicy Creole sauce. Another must-try is the Duck with Mango Sauce, which offers a delicious combination of savory and sweet flavors.

7. Le Jardin d'Epicure (St. Martin)
- Atmosphere: For those seeking a fine-dining experience, Le Jardin d'Epicure is the place to be. Located in the heart of St. Martin, this upscale restaurant offers an intimate, romantic atmosphere with beautiful French-Caribbean decor. It's perfect for an evening out with someone special.

- Pricing: Higher-end pricing with appetizers starting from $15 to $25 USD, main courses from $30 to $50 USD, and desserts from $12 to $20 USD.
- Signature Dishes: The Lobster with Vanilla Sauce is a standout dish, combining the sweetness of lobster with the rich depth of vanilla. They also offer a delicious Roast Lamb with Rosemary and Garlic, which is tender and flavorful.

8. Chez Gaston (Dominican Republic)
- Atmosphere: Located near the port in the Dominican Republic, Chez Gaston offers a relaxed, beachside atmosphere with a cozy, rustic feel. The restaurant is known for its lively vibe, great music, and friendly service, making it ideal for both families and groups of friends.
- Pricing: Affordable, with most appetizers costing between $8 to $15 USD, mains ranging from $18 to $25 USD, and desserts around $5 to $10 USD.
- Signature Dishes: The Mofongo is a must-try—this dish made from mashed plantains, garlic, and pork is a Dominican classic. Pair it with the Pescado a la Parrilla (grilled fish) for a perfect, flavorful meal.

9. The Beach House (Antigua)
- Atmosphere: A casual and vibrant beachside restaurant, The Beach House offers a relaxed vibe with stunning views of the turquoise Caribbean Sea. It's great for a laid-back meal while enjoying the coastal breeze, perfect for both couples and families.
- Pricing: Moderate pricing. Appetizers typically range from $10 to $20 USD, main courses from $20 to $40 USD, and desserts around $8 to $12 USD.

- Signature Dishes: The Grilled Lobster Tail is a must-try, prepared with local herbs and served with a zesty lime butter sauce. You also can't go wrong with their Antiguan Chicken Curry, which is rich, spicy, and comforting.

These restaurants offer an exciting variety of dining experiences, each showcasing local flavors and ingredients. Whether you're seeking fresh seafood, traditional Caribbean dishes, or a sophisticated dining experience, you're sure to find something memorable. Be sure to enjoy a mix of casual beachside meals and gourmet dishes to get the full spectrum of local cuisine.

CHAPTER 10.
CRUISE TIPS FOR FIRST-TIMERS
Maximizing Your Time in Port

When you arrive at a port, it's easy to get overwhelmed by the options of what to do with your limited time. Whether you have a few hours or a full day, it's all about making the most of the time you have. From exploring local attractions to enjoying regional dishes, every moment counts.

Start by planning ahead. Research what the port area and nearby attractions have to offer. A good tip is to find out how long it takes to get to popular sites and if any excursions are offered right at the port. Many cruise ships offer shore excursions that are guided and include transportation, which is a great way to save time and ensure you don't miss anything.

Once you disembark, take a few moments to get your bearings. Some ports have information kiosks where you can grab a map and ask for recommendations. If you're in a city with a public transport system, it's often the quickest and easiest way to get to key areas without the hassle of traffic. If you want a more personal touch, taxis or rideshare services like Uber are also available at most ports.

For those with limited time, pick one or two must-see spots. If you're at a beach destination, nothing beats spending a few hours soaking up the sun, swimming in the clear waters, and enjoying the relaxed pace. Don't forget to sample some local dishes at beachside eateries or small, tucked-away restaurants.

The food is often the heart of the experience, and nothing beats trying something local, especially if it's fresh seafood.

For a more cultural experience, check if there are any museums, historic landmarks, or tours available. You may find hidden gems right near the port that offer a taste of the local history and culture. If you love history, a guided walking tour of the city can introduce you to important sights, from monuments to local markets. Visiting a local market is also a great way to understand the everyday life of the locals, and you can often pick up a souvenir or two.

If you're more adventurous and have more time, consider booking an activity like zip-lining, ATV rides, or hiking through nearby trails. These activities can offer a thrilling way to experience the local landscape, from jungles to mountain views, and give you a different perspective of the region.

Remember to pace yourself. You might be tempted to squeeze in as many activities as possible, but you also want to enjoy the journey and the small moments. If you find a local café or spot with a scenic view, take a break. Relax, sip on a refreshing drink, and just enjoy the surroundings.

When it's time to return to your ship, make sure you plan enough time to get back. You don't want to risk missing the departure, so give yourself an extra 15 to 30 minutes to allow for any unexpected delays, like traffic or last-minute stops.

Maximizing your time in port is all about striking a balance between exploration and relaxation. Focus on what excites you the most, whether it's adventure, culture, or food, and be sure to enjoy the experience without rushing. Keep your plans flexible to account for the unpredictable nature of travel, and take full advantage of your time in the port.

Cruise Etiquette and Safety

When you're on a cruise, it's important to remember that you're sharing the space with many other passengers, and a little etiquette can go a long way to ensure everyone has a pleasant experience. Cruise etiquette is about being respectful of others while also making the most of your time on board and at port. Safety, on the other hand, is essential to keeping everyone protected during the journey.

Start with your cabin. Be mindful of your noise levels, especially during the night. Cruise cabins can be close together, so avoid slamming doors or playing loud music. If you want to chat with friends, try to keep voices low, particularly in hallways or public spaces. Respecting quiet hours ensures that everyone can relax after a long day of exploring or enjoying the ship's amenities.

Dining is another area where etiquette plays a significant role. On cruises, especially during formal dinners, there are usually assigned dining times and seating. If you're in a formal dining setting, dress according to the guidelines provided by the cruise line. This might mean wearing evening attire on certain nights, and casual attire on others. When it comes to food, it's important not to take more than you can eat, as it reduces food waste. Many cruise lines also have buffets where you can return for second helpings, so there's no need to pile up your plate all at once. If you're sitting at a shared table with others, make sure to engage politely and be mindful of their dining preferences and dietary restrictions.

When in public areas, be considerate of others' personal space. Cruise ships have plenty of places to relax, from lounges to pool decks, but it's essential to not occupy spaces that others might want to use, especially when it's crowded. For example, don't leave personal items on deck chairs for extended periods. If you plan to go for a swim or relax by the pool, bring a towel, but only stay in one area and let others have their turn.

When it comes to safety, every cruise line has specific guidelines to ensure the well-being of passengers. First, always listen to the safety briefing at the beginning of your cruise. It's essential to know where your lifeboat station is and how to put on your life vest in case of an emergency. The crew will guide you through these procedures, so don't hesitate to ask any questions.

On board, it's a good idea to familiarize yourself with the ship's layout. Knowing where the elevators, dining areas, and emergency exits are can save you time in case you need to navigate the ship quickly. When you're walking through corridors or up and down stairs, be mindful of your surroundings, especially when the ship is in motion. The seas can be unpredictable, and maintaining your balance is important to avoid accidents.

Safety extends to the shore excursions as well. If you're going on an excursion at a port, ensure that the activities are suitable for your physical abilities. Always follow the guidelines provided by the tour operators, wear any recommended gear (like helmets for ATV rides), and stay within designated areas. If you plan to go swimming, always check the water conditions first and never swim alone.

On the ship, it's important to stay hydrated, especially in warmer climates, and to protect yourself from the sun, whether on deck or ashore. Sunscreen, hats, and staying in the shade when necessary can prevent heatstroke and sunburn. Cruise ships have medical staff on board, but it's always better to be safe than sorry by taking preventive measures.

One of the most important safety tips is to always have your identification and cruise card with you. Your cruise card serves as both your room key and a way to access the ship's services, so make sure it's not lost. It also serves as a lifeline if you need assistance or are in an emergency situation.

Be patient and flexible. Cruises are an incredible way to travel, but sometimes things might not go exactly as planned. There could be weather delays, changes to excursion times, or slight mishaps with bookings. In those moments, being calm and understanding will help everyone, including you, enjoy the experience without added stress.

Cruise etiquette and safety are all about respecting your fellow passengers, taking care of yourself, and ensuring that everyone has an enjoyable and secure journey. A little thoughtfulness can make a big difference in creating a comfortable environment for everyone on board.

CHAPTER 11.
CARIBBEAN CRUISE PLANNER

Sample Itineraries for Different Interests

If you're planning a trip to the Caribbean and want to make the most of your time there, it's helpful to have an itinerary that fits your interests. Whether you're looking for adventure, relaxation, or cultural exploration, there's a perfect itinerary for every type of traveler. Let me share a few sample itineraries based on different interests to help you plan your perfect vacation.

For those seeking adventure, one of the best ways to experience the Caribbean is through a mix of outdoor activities. Start your day with a hike in the morning. In St. Lucia, for example, you can tackle the famous Pitons – two volcanic mountains that offer stunning views from the top. The hike is challenging but worth it, and it's an excellent way to immerse yourself in the island's natural beauty. After the hike, head to the beach for some rest and relaxation. The afternoon is a great time to enjoy water activities like snorkeling or scuba diving. If you're in Grand Cayman, you can snorkel at the famous Stingray City, where you'll have the chance to swim with the friendly stingrays. In the evening, grab a casual dinner at a beachside restaurant, and don't miss the chance to try some local seafood, like fresh fish or conch. You could end your day with a sunset boat tour to unwind while enjoying the island views.

For those interested in exploring local culture and history, a day in Port of Spain, Trinidad, would be an excellent fit. Start with a visit to the National Museum and Art Gallery, where you can learn about the history of the island and its diverse culture. Trinidad has a rich history influenced by African, Indian, and European heritage. After exploring the museum, head to the Queen's Park Savannah, a large park in the center of the city, where you can relax or take a leisurely stroll. From there, you can visit the nearby Royal Botanic Gardens, which is a perfect place to learn about local plants and wildlife. In the afternoon, take a short drive to the Caroni Bird Sanctuary, where you can spot scarlet ibises, Trinidad's national bird. For dinner, try a local restaurant offering traditional dishes like doubles (a type of flatbread filled with chickpeas) or callaloo (a rich vegetable soup).

If you're looking for a more laid-back, relaxing itinerary, spending time on the beaches of the Bahamas is an excellent choice. Start with a leisurely breakfast at your resort, then head to one of the many stunning beaches, like Cable Beach in Nassau, where the white sand and turquoise waters create the perfect setting for a day of sunbathing. You can rent a beach chair and umbrella for comfort, or simply lay out a towel and enjoy the warm sunshine. For lunch, head to a nearby beachside café where you can savor conch fritters or a tropical fruit salad. In the afternoon, enjoy a relaxing boat ride or take a dip in the crystal-clear water. For a unique experience, consider visiting the Exumas, where you can swim with the pigs or explore the underwater cave system at Thunderball Grotto. End your day with a sunset cruise, followed by a delicious dinner at a local restaurant serving Bahamian specialties like rock lobster.

For families traveling with kids, a trip to Puerto Rico offers a fantastic mix of adventure and relaxation, along with plenty of family-friendly activities. Begin your day with a visit to El Yunque National Forest, a lush tropical rainforest where you can hike to waterfalls, like La Mina Falls, and enjoy the beauty of nature. The forest has easy, kid-friendly trails, making it a great option for families. After the hike, head to Luquillo Beach, where you can swim, play in the sand, and enjoy local snacks like "pinchos" (grilled meat skewers) from the food stands. In the afternoon, visit Old San Juan, a historic neighborhood with colorful buildings, cobblestone streets, and forts like El Morro. You can take a guided tour of the fort or simply explore the area on foot, visiting shops and enjoying the local atmosphere. End the day with a family dinner at a waterfront restaurant where you can try traditional Puerto Rican dishes like mofongo (mashed plantains with meat or seafood).

For those who want to immerse themselves in nature and wildlife, a trip to the Dominican Republic offers endless opportunities to explore the island's diverse ecosystems. Begin your day with a visit to Los Haitises National Park, where you can take a boat tour through mangrove forests and see exotic birds like pelicans and herons. The park is known for its unique limestone formations and secluded caves, many of which have ancient Taino cave art. After the tour, head to the famous Bavaro Beach for some downtime. Spend your afternoon snorkeling or diving in the clear waters to see vibrant coral reefs and colorful fish. If you're feeling adventurous, you can even take a trip to Saona Island, a protected nature reserve where you can spot sea turtles and dolphins. For dinner, enjoy fresh seafood at a local beachfront restaurant while watching the sunset over the ocean.

No matter your interest, the Caribbean offers a variety of experiences to suit every type of traveler. By planning an itinerary that aligns with what you enjoy, whether it's outdoor adventure, cultural exploration, beach relaxation, or family fun, you'll be sure to have a memorable time exploring the stunning islands of the Caribbean.

Resources and Useful Links

When planning a trip to the Caribbean, having the right resources and useful links at your fingertips can make your experience much smoother. Whether you're booking flights, finding activities, or looking for tips on local customs, these resources can help you get the most out of your visit.

One of the first places you should visit when planning your Caribbean getaway is official tourism websites for the specific islands you're interested in. These sites often provide up-to-date information on attractions, events, festivals, and must-see sights. They can also give you details on the best times to visit, local weather forecasts, and essential travel tips. Most Caribbean countries have their own tourism websites, where you can find helpful links for accommodations, tours, and transportation options. For example, you can check out sites like Visit Jamaica or Discover Puerto Rico to get a feel for what each destination offers.

For booking flights, there are several search engines that can help you find the best deals. Websites like Google Flights, Kayak, and Skyscanner let you compare prices across different airlines and help you spot promotions. You can also sign up for fare alerts to be notified of price drops. Booking directly with the airline is often a good idea, as you may get better customer service in case you need to make any changes.

When it comes to booking accommodations, sites like Booking.com, Airbnb, and Expedia offer a wide variety of options, from luxury resorts to cozy vacation rentals. These platforms often feature reviews from other travelers, which can help you choose a place that fits your needs. Many accommodations also offer special deals or packages that include activities like excursions, meals, or access to spa services, so be sure to check for those offers.

To find things to do while in the Caribbean, TripAdvisor is a great resource. The site has detailed reviews, photos, and recommendations for tours, restaurants, and activities. You can search by location, category, or activity type, making it easy to find something that suits your interests. Another useful site for excursions is Viator, which offers a range of pre-booked tours, including boat trips, hiking tours, and cultural experiences.

If you're looking for local experiences or unique off-the-beaten-path activities, consider checking out blogs or forums where travelers share their personal recommendations. Websites like Lonely Planet, The Culture Trip, and Atlas Obscura feature hidden gems and insider tips that you might not find in guidebooks. Social media platforms like Instagram and Pinterest can also be helpful for discovering stunning spots that you might want to visit based on photos shared by other travelers.

When traveling to the Caribbean, it's important to stay informed about any health and safety precautions. The Centers for Disease Control and Prevention (CDC) website provides updated travel advisories, vaccination recommendations, and tips on how to stay safe while abroad. You can also check the World Health Organization (WHO) website for global health updates. For more destination-specific health information, visiting local health department websites or talking to your healthcare provider before you go can help you prepare for any specific needs or vaccines.

If you're looking for general information about the Caribbean region, the Caribbean Tourism Organization (CTO) is a fantastic resource. It offers a wealth of information on travel tips, news, and events across multiple islands. The CTO website also has a collection of free travel guides that can give you an overview of the region's culture, history, and must-visit destinations.

With these resources and links, you'll be well-equipped to plan your Caribbean vacation with ease. Whether you're booking your flight, finding local activities, or gathering useful health and safety information, these tools can help you enjoy your time in the Caribbean without any stress.

CHAPTER 12.
PRACTICAL INFORMATION

Money matters and Currency Exchange

When planning a Caribbean cruise, understanding how money works and how to manage your finances on board and in port can make a huge difference in the overall experience. Here's a detailed guide to help you navigate currency exchange and budgeting, ensuring you have a smooth and enjoyable journey.

The currency most commonly used in the Caribbean cruise destinations varies depending on where you're heading, but the Euro (€) is notably significant if you are departing from or visiting Italian cruise ports like Civitavecchia. The Euro is Italy's official currency, and if your cruise starts or ends in Italian ports, understanding its role is key. You'll find that most shops, restaurants, and transportation services accept Euros, but once you venture into other Caribbean islands, you may encounter local currencies like the Eastern Caribbean Dollar (XCD), US Dollar (USD), or other regional currencies. Therefore, it's important to know the local currency of each island you'll visit.

Currency exchange is a crucial part of managing your finances while traveling. In the Caribbean, it's best to exchange your currency at local banks, exchange offices, or ATMs. The currency exchange rates at these locations can vary, so it's wise to shop around before committing to one option. Banks generally offer favorable rates, though they may charge a small fee for the exchange. ATMs are widely available in most

Caribbean ports and will typically allow you to withdraw local currency at a competitive exchange rate. However, be mindful of withdrawal fees, which can be high depending on your bank, so check with your financial institution before traveling. Exchange offices can also be convenient but often come with less favorable rates and higher commissions. If possible, try to avoid exchanging money at the cruise port itself, as these can have inflated rates designed for tourists.

When it comes to budgeting for your Caribbean cruise, it's important to have a realistic idea of the costs involved in your trip. If you're on a budget, you can expect to spend around $50 to $100 per day on basic expenses like meals, local transport, and entry to attractions. Mid-range travelers, seeking a bit more comfort, might budget between $100 to $200 a day, which allows for some more luxurious meals, private tours, or perhaps a day at the beach with rental equipment. Luxury travelers can easily spend upwards of $300 per day, especially if they're indulging in high-end dining, private excursions, or spa experiences. Accommodation is often included in your cruise fare, but if you're staying in a hotel pre- or post-cruise, you can expect to pay around $100 to $250 a night for mid-range hotels, and upwards of $300 a night for luxury resorts, especially in sought-after locations like the Virgin Islands or the Bahamas. For meals, street food or local cafes can cost as little as $5 to $10, while mid-range restaurants might charge $20 to $50 per person for a meal. Onboard cruise ships, meals are often included, though specialty restaurants or drinks can add to your daily costs.

Payment methods are another key consideration when cruising through the Caribbean. Most establishments, both on the cruise and in port, accept credit and debit cards, particularly major ones like Visa and MasterCard. American Express is less widely accepted in some places, so it's always a good idea to double-check before relying on it. Also, consider bringing a prepaid travel card or local payment apps like Apple Pay or Google Pay, which are becoming more commonly accepted in many Caribbean destinations. Still, it's important to carry some cash for smaller purchases like souvenirs at local markets, or when visiting remote areas where card payment isn't an option. Having a mix of payment methods ensures you're always prepared for any situation.

While prices in the Caribbean can vary by destination, a few general trends are worth noting. Peak tourist seasons, such as during the winter holidays or spring break, can drive up the cost of accommodations, dining, and activities. You might find that off-peak months, like late spring or early fall, offer better deals and fewer crowds. Popular tourist spots can often be pricier than local hangouts. For example, you might find that a beachfront restaurant in a busy tourist area like Nassau or St. Thomas charges higher prices for the same meal you could get for half the price at a local spot a few streets away. Exploring less-commercialized areas often yields more affordable options. Additionally, don't forget about hidden costs like service charges, tips, or additional fees for amenities like Wi-Fi or beach loungers, which can add up if you're not careful.

I remember my first Caribbean cruise, when I was a bit overwhelmed with managing my budget on board and in port.

I had assumed that everything would be covered by the cruise package, but when I arrived at a stunning beach in St. Kitts, I realized that renting snorkeling gear and using the beach facilities wasn't included. I hadn't thought to check beforehand, and it left me scrambling to exchange a bit more cash. From that experience, I learned to always double-check what's included and ensure that I carry extra local currency for these small, unexpected costs.

To make managing money easier, I recommend using apps like Mint or Travel Mapper to keep track of your spending. These apps help you monitor your budget in real time, so you don't end up overspending. Currency converter apps like XE are also handy, especially when you need to check exchange rates on the go. For more detailed information on expenses, websites like Numbeo provide valuable insights into the cost of living in various Caribbean destinations, helping you plan more effectively.

By keeping these tips in mind, you'll be able to handle money matters smoothly while cruising through the Caribbean, allowing you to focus more on the beauty and excitement of your trip, and less on the stress of managing your finances.

Language and Communication

When preparing for a Caribbean cruise, it's important to understand the languages spoken in the region and how to communicate effectively while on your travels. While English is the primary language spoken in many Caribbean islands, a cruise departing from Italian or German-speaking ports, such as Civitavecchia in Italy, brings a different dynamic. The main languages in this case are Italian and German, and it's helpful to familiarize yourself with some basic phrases in these languages. Understanding these languages will enhance your experience both onboard and during your excursions at various destinations. In addition to Italian and German, you may also encounter regional dialects in the Caribbean islands, which can range from Jamaican Patois to Haitian Creole. However, English remains widely spoken, especially in tourist areas.

To make your interactions smoother, here are some essential greetings and polite phrases in Italian and German that will help you get by during your cruise. For instance, in Italian, "Ciao" (pronounced "chow") means "hello" or "hi," and is commonly used in both formal and informal settings. "Buongiorno" (pronounced "bwohn-jor-no") means "good morning," while "Buonasera" (pronounced "bwoh-nah-seh-rah") means "good evening." In German, you can use "Hallo" (pronounced "hah-loh") for "hello," "Guten Morgen" (pronounced "goo-ten mohr-gen") for "good morning," and "Guten Abend" (pronounced "goo-ten ah-bent") for "good evening." To express politeness, "per favore" (pronounced "per fah-voh-ray") in Italian means "please," and "grazie" (pronounced "graht-see-eh") means "thank you." In German, "bitte" (pronounced "bi-teh") is the equivalent of "please," and "danke" (pronounced "dahn-keh") is used for "thank you." "Excuse me" in Italian is "scusa" (pronounced "skoo-zah") and in German, it's "Entschuldigung" (pronounced "ent-shool-dee-goong").

For travelers who may need to navigate practical situations, here are a few helpful phrases in both languages. When ordering food, in Italian, you can say "Vorrei il menu, per favore" (pronounced "vor-ray eel meh-noo, per fah-voh-ray") to ask for the menu, while in German, you can ask "Haben Sie die Speisekarte?" (pronounced "hah-ben zee dee shpye-zuh-kar-teh"). If you're seeking directions, "Dove si trova la stazione?" (pronounced "doh-veh see troh-vah lah stah-tsyo-neh") means "Where is the station?" in Italian, and "Wo ist der Bahnhof?" (pronounced "voh ist dair bahn-hoff") means "Where is the train station?" in German. To make purchases, you can say "Quanto costa?" (pronounced "kwan-toh koh-stah") for "How much does it cost?" in Italian, and in German, you can ask "Wie viel kostet das?" (pronounced "vee feel kohs-teht dahs?"). If you need assistance, "Mi può aiutare?" (pronounced "mee pwah ah-yoo-tah-ray") in Italian means "Can you help me?" and in German, you can say "Könnten Sie mir helfen?" (pronounced "ker-nten zee meer hel-fen").

For those who want to quickly pick up these essential phrases before their cruise, there are several resources to help you. Mobile apps like Duolingo and Babbel offer interactive lessons that make learning Italian and German easy and fun. For more in-depth learning, apps like Memrise and Anki also provide flashcards and spaced repetition to reinforce vocabulary and phrases. If you prefer a more traditional approach, carrying a small phrasebook tailored to travel in Europe or the Caribbean can be a handy reference. There are even specific phrasebooks for cruising that can help you navigate not only language barriers but cultural differences as well.

Communication is not just about words; it's also about understanding the local culture and etiquette. In many Caribbean ports, as well as on European cruise ships, body language and eye contact are essential. In general, Italian and German speakers appreciate good manners, so make sure to greet people with a friendly smile and a proper "Buongiorno" or "Guten Morgen" when interacting with locals. While you're on a Caribbean cruise, the crew is usually multilingual, and you'll find English-speaking staff members at hotels, restaurants, and major tourist attractions. But showing effort in speaking the local language, even just a few words, is always appreciated and helps foster a deeper connection with the people you meet.

Finally, it's important to respect the languages and cultures of the places you visit. While English may be the most common language across Caribbean islands, learning a few words of Italian or German can be a small gesture of goodwill that can go a long way. Locals appreciate travelers who make the effort to communicate in their native language, and it's a sign of respect for their culture. Whether you're ordering gelato in an Italian port or asking for directions to a market in a Caribbean town, taking the time to learn and use basic phrases can make your cruise experience even more rewarding. By embracing the local languages, you not only improve your chances of having more meaningful interactions but also show respect for the communities you're visiting.

In conclusion, while you don't need to be fluent in Italian or German to enjoy your Caribbean cruise, learning some basic phrases and understanding the local language customs will make your experience smoother and more enjoyable. From ordering meals to navigating ports, these simple phrases will help you connect with the people around you and fully embrace the culture and hospitality of the regions you're visiting.

Safety and Health

When planning a Caribbean cruise, your safety and health should always be top priorities. With the right precautions and knowledge, you can make the most of your adventure while staying safe and healthy. Here's a guide to help you navigate the beautiful Caribbean with confidence.

General safety tips for travelers on a Caribbean cruise start with being aware of your surroundings. Always stay alert, especially in unfamiliar areas, whether you're on the ship or exploring a port of call. It's a good idea to avoid poorly lit areas after dark and stay in well-populated places. If you're in a busy port, consider traveling in groups or with a guide. Respecting local customs and traditions is also important for building rapport with locals and avoiding misunderstandings. For example, some Caribbean islands may have specific cultural practices or dress codes that are important to follow, so it's worth doing a little research before you travel.

If you're planning outdoor activities like hiking, snorkeling, or exploring nature trails, there are additional safety precautions to consider. For hiking, always check the weather conditions before heading out, as tropical storms can be sudden and intense. Make sure to choose trails that are suitable for your fitness level and carry enough water and snacks. Be aware of trail markers, and don't stray from the path. If you're venturing into higher altitudes, such as hiking on mountain trails, it's important to recognize symptoms of altitude sickness, which can include dizziness, nausea, and shortness of breath. If you experience these symptoms, descend to a lower altitude immediately and seek medical help if needed.

Health precautions are essential in the Caribbean, given the hot and humid climate. Staying hydrated is crucial, especially if you're out exploring in the sun for long periods. Carry a refillable water bottle and drink regularly to avoid dehydration. The sun can be intense, so applying sunscreen with a high SPF is a must, even on cloudy days. It's also wise to wear protective clothing, such as hats and sunglasses, and seek shade when the sun is at its strongest. When it comes to clothing, dress in layers to accommodate for changing weather conditions. Light, breathable fabrics are perfect for hot days, while a light jacket may come in handy if temperatures drop at night. Additionally, check with your doctor before your trip to ensure you're up to date on vaccinations, especially for diseases like hepatitis A and typhoid, which can be more common in tropical areas.

In case of emergencies, it's helpful to have a list of important contacts on hand. Each island has its own emergency services number, but the general emergency number in many Caribbean islands is 911, similar to the United States. Be sure to know the nearest hospital or medical facility, and if you're planning outdoor activities like hiking or exploring remote areas, research any local rescue services, such as coast guard or mountain rescue. For example, the Virgin Islands have a specific number for their National Park Service's emergency response team, and other islands may have similar services for visitors in need. Make sure your cruise ship has a plan for medical evacuations in case of a serious emergency.

Obtaining travel insurance is one of the best ways to protect yourself in the event of unexpected circumstances. A good travel insurance policy should cover medical expenses, including evacuation costs, and offer 24/7 emergency assistance. It's also wise to check if the policy covers activities such as hiking, scuba diving, or any other adventure activities you're planning to do. When shopping for travel insurance, look for policies that offer cancellation protection and coverage for lost baggage as well.

In the Caribbean, local health services are generally accessible in most tourist areas. Pharmacies and clinics are available for basic health needs like prescription refills, over-the-counter medications, and minor injuries. Some larger islands have private healthcare facilities, while smaller islands may rely on government-run clinics. Before traveling, check the availability of medical services on your specific ports of call and know the nearest medical centers. It's also a good idea to carry a small health kit with you, including basic medications like pain relievers, insect repellent, and any personal prescriptions you may need.

To help stay informed and safe during your trip, there are several resources and tools you can use. Apps like Travel Smart by the International SOS provide helpful travel health advice and emergency contact information. Other apps, such as the Red Cross First Aid app, can give you instant access to first aid procedures in case of an emergency. The CDC website is another valuable resource, offering up-to-date information on health advisories, including vaccination recommendations and disease outbreaks in the Caribbean. Additionally, your cruise line will likely have an app or website with information about onboard safety and medical services.

By being prepared and following these health and safety tips, you'll ensure that your Caribbean cruise is both enjoyable and safe. From staying hydrated and sun-safe to knowing emergency contacts and investing in good travel insurance, these steps will help you navigate the Caribbean with confidence. Whether you're hiking through rainforests, enjoying the beautiful beaches, or exploring local culture, prioritizing safety and health will allow you to experience the best the Caribbean has to offer.

Emergency Contacts

When traveling to the Caribbean, it's important to be aware of emergency services and know what to do in case of an unexpected situation. The Caribbean is a beautiful and diverse region, but like anywhere else, emergencies can happen. Whether you're in a busy city or a remote area, being prepared can make all the difference.

Emergency services in the Caribbean vary by island and region, but most of the larger and more developed areas have reliable police, fire, and medical services. In urban areas, you will find well-equipped hospitals, police stations, and fire departments, while more rural and remote areas may have limited resources, but emergency services still exist, albeit with longer response times. It's always a good idea to familiarize yourself with the services available in the area you're visiting, as the level of access may differ from place to place.

For general emergencies across the Caribbean, the number to call is usually 911, much like in North America. However, depending on the island or country, some places may have their own specific emergency numbers for police, fire, or medical services. Knowing these numbers can help you get the quickest response.

The key emergency numbers you should have on hand include the general emergency number, local police, ambulance services, fire department, and, if you're planning to be in more mountainous or remote areas, mountain rescue services.

Always have these numbers saved in your phone and written down in case you need to refer to them quickly.

While emergency services are accessible, it's helpful to know where the nearest hospitals and clinics are in the places you'll be visiting. In major cities and tourist hubs like Nassau in the Bahamas, San Juan in Puerto Rico, and Kingston in Jamaica, you'll find large hospitals with modern facilities. For example, the Doctors Hospital in Nassau (Bahamas) provides comprehensive medical care, while the Puerto Rico Medical Center in San Juan is one of the largest hospitals in the region, equipped for emergencies. Be sure to carry a list of local hospitals or clinics in the area where you'll be staying, and know their contact numbers and addresses.

In case of an emergency, it's crucial to stay calm and follow these basic steps: First, assess the situation and call for help using the appropriate emergency number. Be prepared to give your exact location, any relevant details about the emergency, and a description of the situation. If language is a barrier, try to communicate as clearly as possible, using simple words and gestures. If you don't speak the local language, many emergency responders in the Caribbean can understand basic English, especially in more tourist-heavy areas. However, it's always a good idea to learn a few key phrases in the local language to help in an emergency. For example, "Help!" or "Call an ambulance" is useful in any language.

Travel insurance that covers medical emergencies, evacuations, and repatriation is one of the most important things to have when traveling abroad. Many insurance providers offer travel assistance services that can help you find local hospitals or medical services and even arrange medical evacuations if necessary. Be sure to have your insurance details easily accessible and know how to contact the 24-hour emergency assistance number provided by your insurer.

When it comes to outdoor activities like hiking or excursions in more remote areas, preparation is key. Always carry a first aid kit, ensure your phone is fully charged, and inform someone of your plans before heading out. This way, if something goes wrong, someone will know where to find you. If you're hiking in a mountainous area or visiting remote beaches, let your hotel or a local guide know your expected return time, and always stay on marked paths to avoid getting lost.

Culturally, locals in the Caribbean are generally very helpful and welcoming, but it's important to be respectful when asking for assistance. In some areas, people may not be familiar with tourist-related emergencies, so being polite and patient can help you get the assistance you need. A friendly approach will go a long way, and offering a small tip for someone helping in an emergency situation is appreciated.

I remember a time when I was on a small island in the Caribbean, and I had an unfortunate accident while exploring a hiking trail. I twisted my ankle and found myself far from any main roads or towns. Luckily, I had a guide with me, and we were able to contact the local emergency number for help. The rescue team arrived relatively quickly, but it made me realize how important it is to always let someone know your plans, stay prepared, and keep emergency numbers handy.

To help with staying informed and prepared during your trip, consider downloading emergency apps that provide local emergency information, such as the Red Cross emergency app or the local government app for the Caribbean island you are visiting. These can give you real-time information on what to do in case of an emergency, local health advisories, and much more.

In summary, staying safe and knowing how to handle an emergency in the Caribbean is essential for any traveler. By familiarizing yourself with emergency contact numbers, having a plan for medical emergencies, ensuring you have travel insurance, and staying prepared for outdoor activities, you can enjoy your trip with peace of mind. And remember, kindness, patience, and respect go a long way when seeking help in a foreign place.

Useful Websites and Apps

When planning a Caribbean cruise, the right apps can make your journey more enjoyable and stress-free. With the vast array of destinations, activities, and services available, these apps can help you plan, navigate, and enjoy every aspect of your trip. Whether you're exploring tropical islands, booking accommodations, or hiking through scenic landscapes, the following apps are indispensable for making the most of your Caribbean cruise.

One of the most essential apps to have is a transportation app. Whether you're navigating public transport, booking taxis, or renting a car, apps like Uber, Lyft, or local taxi services in specific Caribbean destinations can save you time and hassle. For cruises, the cruise line's official app is another key tool to download, as it provides real-time updates on itineraries, excursion bookings, dining reservations, and even onboard activities.

For outdoor enthusiasts, apps like AllTrails and Gaia GPS are perfect for planning and navigating hikes in the Caribbean. The Caribbean offers some amazing hiking trails, from the lush rainforests of Puerto Rico to the volcanic landscapes of St. Lucia. AllTrails provides trail maps, difficulty levels, and reviews from other hikers, while Gaia GPS allows you to track your hike using offline maps, which is especially useful in more remote areas. For additional weather forecasts and navigation, ViewRanger is another excellent app that offers GPS-enabled trails and weather updates. These apps ensure you are always prepared for your outdoor adventures, helping you stay safe and on track.

When it comes to accommodation and dining, apps like Booking.com, Airbnb, and TripAdvisor are essential for finding places to stay and eat. Booking.com offers a wide selection of hotels and resorts, complete with guest reviews and booking options. Airbnb provides unique accommodations like beachfront properties and villas, perfect for those seeking a more personalized stay. TripAdvisor is a fantastic tool for browsing dining options, checking reviews, and booking reservations, whether you're looking for a fine-dining experience or a laid-back beachside café. All these apps allow you to compare prices, read real reviews from fellow travelers, and make your arrangements with ease.

Language barriers can sometimes be an obstacle, but with apps like Google Translate, Duolingo, and iTranslate, you can easily communicate with locals. Google Translate can help you translate signs, menus, and even conversations in real-time, making it an essential tool when you don't speak the local language. Duolingo is perfect for learning the basics of the language before your trip, allowing you to pick up common phrases and greetings. iTranslate offers text and voice translations, which can be useful for both written and verbal communication, helping you navigate different dialects across the Caribbean islands.

In case of an emergency or to stay safe, there are several apps that can be life-savers. The First Aid app by the American Red Cross provides step-by-step guidance on dealing with medical emergencies, from cuts and burns to heart attacks. GeoSure Travel Safety offers real-time safety scores for various regions, helping you assess the safety of the areas you're visiting. Additionally, having travel insurance apps that provide emergency contact numbers, health advisories, and evacuation assistance can give you peace of mind throughout your trip.

For those interested in learning more about the culture and history of the Caribbean, there are apps like Dolomiti UNESCO, which showcases cultural heritage sites, and audio guides for museums and historical sites across the region. These apps allow you to explore the rich history, art, and culture of the islands through guided tours and insightful commentary. Additionally, walking tour apps often provide self-guided tours that take you to hidden gems, enriching your experience as you wander through Caribbean towns and cities.

One of the most important features to consider when choosing apps for your Caribbean cruise is offline capability. Many parts of the Caribbean, especially more remote islands, have limited or expensive internet access. Apps like Maps.me allow you to download maps for offline use, ensuring you won't get lost when you're away from Wi-Fi. You can also download essential guides, weather reports, and even trail maps in advance, so you're always prepared. Be sure to download the necessary resources before your trip, so you have access even without an internet connection.

When downloading and using apps, it's important to ensure your device stays charged, especially since you'll likely be relying on it for navigation and communication. Carry a portable charger or power bank to keep your phone topped up during excursions. Also, be mindful of roaming charges and data usage when traveling internationally. To avoid hefty charges, consider downloading apps that allow you to use them offline, or purchase an international data plan if necessary.

In summary, the right apps can enhance your Caribbean cruise experience in countless ways, from navigating transportation and accommodations to exploring the great outdoors and staying safe. By preparing ahead of time and downloading useful apps before your trip, you'll have everything you need at your fingertips to make your journey as smooth and enjoyable as possible. Whether you're hiking a mountain, translating a menu, or finding the best local restaurant, these apps are your ultimate travel companions.

CONCLUSION

As you embark on your Caribbean cruise, you'll soon discover the magic that makes this region so unique and special. The Caribbean is a place where vibrant cultures meet natural beauty, where the lush green hills, crystal-clear waters, and golden beaches create a canvas for adventure. From the excitement of exploring historic towns to the thrill of snorkeling over coral reefs, the Caribbean cruise offers a perfect blend of outdoor exploration, rich cultural experiences, and tantalizing culinary delights. Each island you visit brings its own charm, whether it's the lively music of Cuba, the colonial architecture of Puerto Rico, or the serene landscapes of the Virgin Islands. It's a region that promises both relaxation and excitement, whether you're lounging on a beach with a cold drink in hand or taking part in a high-energy adventure like zip-lining through the jungle.

I'll always remember my first encounter with the Caribbean – the sound of steel drums echoing through the air as I strolled through a bustling local market. The colorful stalls, filled with fresh tropical fruits and hand-crafted goods, created an atmosphere that was both lively and inviting. That moment, filled with laughter and vibrant colors, truly captured the essence of the Caribbean. This experience reminded me of the immense beauty of this region, not just in its landscapes but also in the warmth and generosity of its people. The Caribbean is more than just a place to visit; it's a place to connect, to embrace adventure, and to appreciate the wonders of nature in a way that's hard to find anywhere else.

For those of you reading this, I encourage you to step outside your comfort zone and dive into the Caribbean's many offerings. It's easy to get comfortable lounging on a beach, but the real rewards come from stepping into the unknown. Try hiking a challenging trail, like the famous El Yunque Rainforest in Puerto Rico, where the tropical plants and cascading waterfalls will make every step worth it. Taste the local dishes, like jerk chicken in Jamaica or fresh seafood in Barbados, and savor the flavors that reflect the island's soul. Engage with the locals – you'll be surprised how much a simple conversation can enrich your understanding of the culture and make you feel even more connected to the place. It's these moments that will leave you with unforgettable memories and a deeper appreciation for the world around you.

While the major tourist spots in the Caribbean are certainly worth visiting, don't forget to venture off the beaten path. Seek out the hidden gems, the quieter beaches, the charming villages tucked away from the crowds. It's in these places that you'll discover the true spirit of the islands. You might stumble upon a secluded bay where you're the only one in sight, or find a small family-run café serving the best dish you've ever tasted. These experiences, though less commercialized, are often the ones that stay with you long after you've returned home.

As you explore, keep in mind the importance of sustainable travel practices. The Caribbean is an extraordinary place, but it's also one that's vulnerable to the impacts of tourism. Respect the environment by avoiding plastic, supporting local businesses, and being mindful of your ecological footprint. When you engage in responsible tourism, you're helping to ensure that the Caribbean remains a beautiful and thriving destination for generations to come.

To make the most of your Caribbean cruise, plan ahead but also leave room for spontaneity. Sometimes, the best experiences come from unexpected encounters or last-minute decisions, whether it's a boat ride with new friends or stumbling upon a local festival. Don't be afraid to ask locals for recommendations; they know the best places to eat, explore, and experience the true essence of their islands. A little bit of curiosity and openness can take you to places that guidebooks can't.

As you embark on your journey, remember that the Caribbean isn't just a vacation destination – it's an opportunity to embrace adventure, create lasting memories, and connect with a culture that's as rich as the blue waters surrounding it. I invite you to share your experiences, whether through social media or travel blogs, because the stories we tell are what help to preserve the magic of places like the Caribbean. Your adventure, your memories, and your reflections are all part of a global tapestry that inspires and connects travelers from around the world.

In the end, the beauty of travel lies in its ability to open our hearts, stretch our limits, and bring us closer to the world. The Caribbean cruise experience offers all of this and more. So, go ahead, embrace the adventure ahead. Let the vibrant colors, the rhythm of the music, and the warmth of the people inspire you. The memories you create here will last a lifetime – a reminder of the joy that comes from discovering new places, meeting new people, and immersing yourself in the wonders of the world.

MAP
Scan QR Code with device to view map for easy navigation

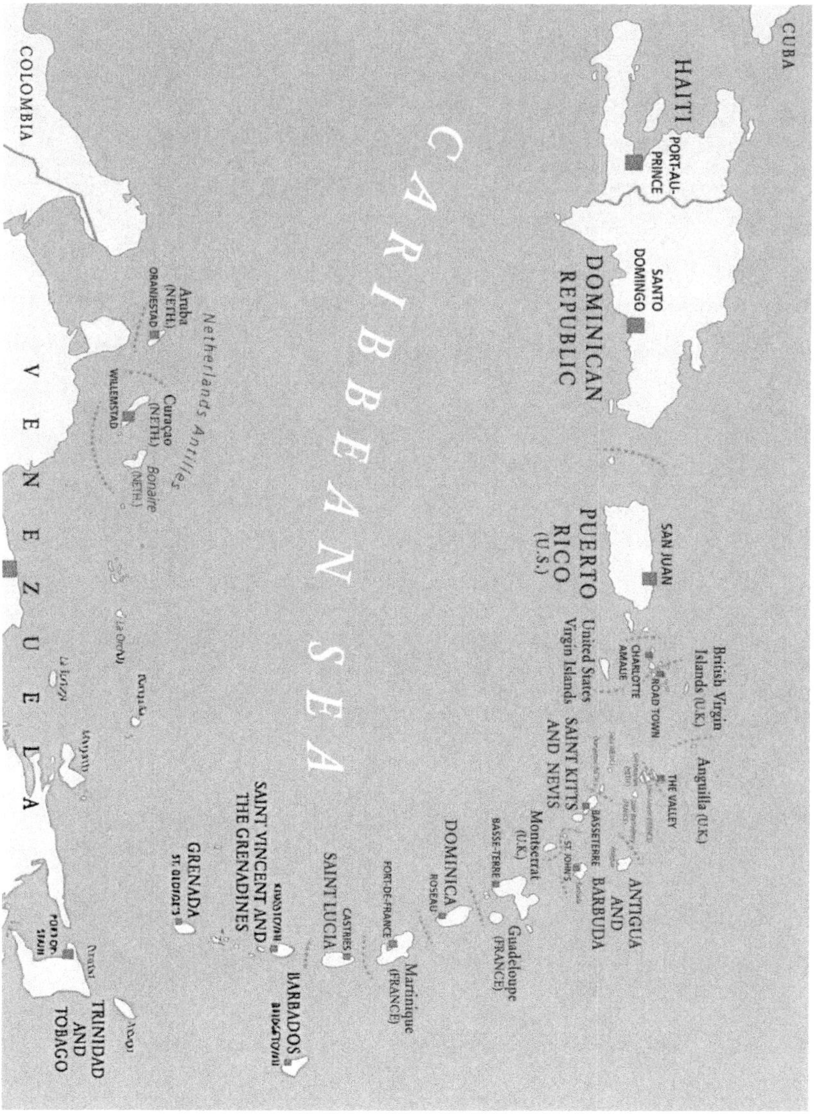
CUBA
HAITI
PORT-AU-PRINCE
SANTO DOMINGO
DOMINICAN REPUBLIC
CARIBBEAN SEA
SAN JUAN
PUERTO RICO (U.S.)
British Virgin Islands (U.K.)
ROAD TOWN
CHARLOTTE AMALIE
United States Virgin Islands
Anguilla (U.K.)
THE VALLEY
SAINT KITTS AND NEVIS
BASSETERRE
ST. JOHN'S
ANTIGUA AND BARBUDA
Montserrat (U.K.)
BASSE-TERRE
Guadeloupe (FRANCE)
DOMINICA
ROSEAU
FORT-DE-FRANCE
Martinique (FRANCE)
CASTRIES
SAINT LUCIA
SAINT VINCENT AND THE GRENADINES
BARBADOS
GRENADA
TRINIDAD AND TOBAGO
Aruba (NETH.)
ORANJESTAD
Curaçao (NETH.)
WILLEMSTAD
Bonaire (NETH.)
Netherlands Antilles
COLOMBIA
VENEZUELA

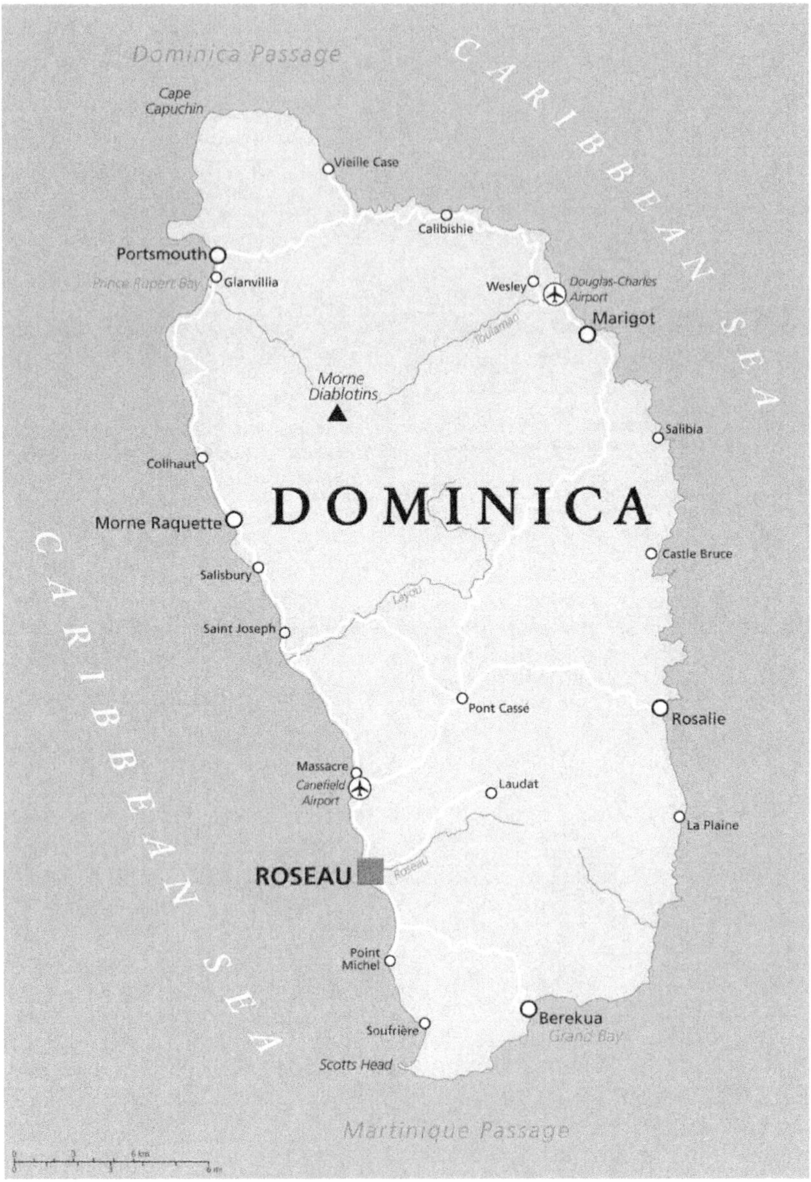
Dominica Passage
CARIBBEAN SEA
Cape Capuchin
Vieille Case
Calibishie
Portsmouth
Prince Rupert Bay
Glanvillia
Wesley
Douglas-Charles Airport
Marigot
Toulaman
Morne Diablotins
Salibia
Colihaut
DOMINICA
Morne Raquette
Castle Bruce
Salisbury
Layou
Saint Joseph
CARIBBEAN SEA
Pont Cassé
Rosalie
Massacre
Canefield Airport
Laudat
La Plaine
ROSEAU
Roseau
Point Michel
Berekua
Grand Bay
Soufrière
Scotts Head
Martinique Passage

NOTES

Date:

NOTES

Date:

NOTES

NOTES

Date:

NOTES

NOTES

Date: